Praise

MW00943876

"DeeAnn Jeremiah invites us to put down the heavy weight of expectation and take off our mask of perfection in favor of authentic Christian community and a deeper trust in the goodness of God. Readers will be encouraged, challenged and moved by the real-life stories of the homeless friends who inspired DeeAnn to dig deeper into her life-long preconceptions about what it means to be a "good" Christian. With vulnerability, honesty, humor and thorough research, DeeAnn shares the story of how God led her to a place of healing and wholeness, and offers guidance to others seeking freedom from the confines of Christian image. Read *Imagine*, take a deep breath, and step into the freedom and joy God is offering!"

Kelly Johnson, MSW
Author of Being Brave: A 40 Day Journey to the Life
God Dreams for You
Author, Speaker, Co-Active Coach
Board Chair, The Lamb Center

"As a therapist it is extremely important to understand the context and impact of trauma as the root of many emotional and psychological difficulties as well as internal conflict and confusion. To ignore this element of an individual's story is to ignore their story altogether.

With biblical depth and vulnerability, Jeremiah acknowledges these stories, as well as her own, with tenderness and honesty. You can almost hear her whisper 'I see you' to each character and with every turn of a chapter.

Jeremiah is a powerful storyteller who opens a window into the ugly and scary truth of image and brokenness while simultaneously revealing what it can teach us about hope, compassion, love, healing and faith.

In my work, I listen to Millennials express confusion, concern and sometimes outright terror about the future and what they are supposed to do, who they are supposed to be and how to get what everyone else has got. Image over everything. No wonder so many adolescents, young adults and even older adults are so confused.

Jeremiah encourages and inspires her readers to press in, dig in, and *go there* in order to discover how our cultural norms, faith, values, childhood, and personal experiences have shaped our image of ourselves and reinforce the image we struggle to portray. *Imagine* teaches us to reach our destiny, as God intended."

Kathryn Robertson, LCPC
Senior Counselor, Division of Child and Adolescent
Psychiatry, University of Maryland

"DeeAnn takes a very courageous 'deep dive' into her journey with Christ—sharing transparently. The catalyst for her story are the very rich experiences with the poor and homeless gained while being part of God's transforming work at The Lamb Center. This will inspire you to both confront your own brokenness and embrace God's loving mercy extended to everyone."

Larry Huff
CEO, Samaritan Inns

"It is often said that we live best when we examine our lives—against God's Word, the world around us, and seek ways to change for the better. Stripping away all pretense and looking for the real person we were meant to be, created to be, for God's purpose and glory. In *Imagine*, DeeAnn shares her own unique journey of personal transformation gleaned from volunteering at a daytime homeless shelter. As you meet the various clients she serves, and learn of their stories, DeeAnn candidly unpacks her own story of moving beyond pain to healing, embracing a new life and purpose. I found DeeAnn's transparency so refreshing in a culture that promotes anything but the real and raw of life. *Imagine* provides a platform for rich discussion with questions to ponder throughout. I envision using it with my teams that serve regularly in the inner city and in our spiritual mentoring ministry. Powerful in its offering of self-examination, any group would benefit from using this as the basis of a study."

Deedee Collins
Deacon, Missions & Outreach
Coordinator, Women's Spiritual Mentoring Ministry
Immanuel Bible Church, Springfield, Virginia
Board of Directors, Central Union Mission,
Washington, D.C.

"DeeAnn weaves her tender and vulnerable story through a real life experience of heartache and determined hope. How refreshing her honesty! How life giving her view and experience of God and His love for her and all of us! Just imagine! This book will leave you to ponder your own circumstances and also to imagine how free you could be if you were to yield and surrender your true self to our great God."

Rose Zacharias Meeder, MD
ER physician & podcaster,
Intersection...where real life and faith collide
www.iwrzm.com

"Radical. Dramatic. Positive. Change. If this is what you're looking for, then *Imagine* is for you! DeeAnn Jeremiah clearly communicates what it takes to get to *real* abundant life. *Imagine* is a must read for all who are seriously *tired of fake* and want to lay hold of the purposeful, dynamic, adventurous life to which God calls us all. I encourage you to turn the page…your Destiny awaits!"

Karen Duckett
Founder, Rescued for Destiny - Joel 2 Army
Co-host/producer, Vital Force

"*Imagine* is a book for anyone who yearns to be *real* and understand what it is to live a truly Christ-centered life. *Imagine* tells DeeAnn's story of understanding God's message for us through the story of others, the clients she meets at the Lamb Center.

DeeAnn writes from a narrative perspective, challenging our preconceived notions about people who are homeless. The stories she tells reminds us we are all more than our marginalizing stories. DeeAnn paints a picture of healing by using relevant passages from the Bible as well as references to innumerable books that helped her peel away the layers of fake that were keeping her from getting real.

I couldn't put it down! What a read for anyone who values being real, living a Christ-centered life, and cutting through the nonsense of our religious traditions. What I love is that while sharing her story, the story of others opens God's message to us—a tricky goal, but done masterfully!

A sentence from the final chapter says it all: 'Imagine! Participating with the God of the universe in His plans and purposes for us and the world. It doesn't get any better than that.'"

Carol Kaffenberger, Ph.D.
Associate Professor Emerita
Counseling & Development, George Mason University

"If you feel bound or feel like there's something missing at church, you need to read *Imagine*. Christ promised that He was going to set the captives free. Men, in their own desire and in their own selfishness, often try to make other men captive to something, even if it's just to an idea of the way things should be done. However, that's not what Christ said to do. *Imagine* addresses the traditions of men which are not of God, and more, and reading it will lead you to freedom."

Timothy Duckett
Co-host/producer, Vital Force

"DeeAnn's authenticity is medicine to the disenchanted heart! In *Imagine*, she takes the reader through her painful journey with Christian culture and the healing she found as she dismantled her concern for the way others told her things *should* be and replaced it with God's truth. She dares to venture into hard topics and ask questions that so many, those inside and outside of the Church, have wrestled with.

Much of the learning and healing that DeeAnn writes about happened around the table at a homeless day shelter called The Lamb Center. As she invites us to hear the stories of the real individuals who touched her life, we get the feeling that we are right there with her at that table, where no questions are turned away, no circumstances are too ugly, and no masks are required. *Imagine* is a book that is fair, honest, wise, and balanced. It is both comforting and refreshing."

Brittany Clarke
Editor and writer
brittclarke.com

Elena, Ren + Ann,
You are amazingly
friends + neighbors!
Follow God
wherever He
leads!

IMAGINE

♡ Dee Jen
Jeremiah

IMAGINE

Stripping Christian Image and Living God's Abundant Real Life

BY
DEEANN JOY JEREMIAH

Xulon Elite

Xulon Press Elite
2301 Lucien Way #415
Maitland, FL 32751
407.339.4217
www.xulonpress.com

© 2018 by DeeAnn Joy Jeremiah

All rights reserved solely by the author. The author guarantees all contents are original and do not infringe upon the legal rights of any other person or work. No part of this book may be reproduced in any form without the permission of the author. The views expressed in this book are not necessarily those of the publisher.

Unless otherwise indicated, Scripture quotations taken from the Holy Bible, New International Version® (NIV). Copyright © 1973, 1978, 1984 by Biblica, Inc.™. Used by permission of Zondervan. All rights reserved.

Scripture quotations taken from the Amplified Bible (AMP). Copyright © 1954, 1958, 1962, 1964, 1965, 1987, 2015 by The Lockman Foundation. Used by permission. All rights reserved.

Scripture quotations taken from the New King James Version® (NKJV). Copyright © 1982 by Thomas Nelson, Inc. Used by permission. All rights reserved.

Scripture quotations taken from the Holy Bible, New Living Translation (NLT). Copyright ©1996, 2004 by Tyndale House Foundation. Used by permission of Tyndale House Publishers, Inc.

Scripture quotations taken from The Message (MSG). Copyright © 1993, 1994, 1995, 1996, 2000. Used by permission of NavPress Publishing Group. Used by permission. All rights reserved.

Printed in the United States of America.

ISBN-13: 9781545624258

Events described are based on DeeAnn Jeremiah's memory, whether accurate or inaccurate, of real-world situations. However, the names and descriptions of all homeless guests have been changed. Some events have been compressed, and some dialogue has been recreated. Any resemblance to persons living or dead resulting from changes to names or identifying details is entirely coincidental and unintentional.

For the homeless and homeless at heart;
For the poor and the poor in spirit

In memory and honor of Beverly Isaak Klassen
Mother, Friend, Believer, and now Seer
1934 – 2015

Now we see things imperfectly, like puzzling reflections in a mirror, but then we will see everything with perfect clarity. All that I know now is partial and incomplete, but then I will know everything completely, just as God now knows me completely. (1 Corinthians 13:12 NLT)

Table of Contents

Foreword

*J*esus came so that we may have life and have it abundantly. Oftentimes, the false "image" we have of ourselves keeps us from living this abundant life. As we journey through the messy and painful twists and turns of life, we often protect our deep wounds and hurts by projecting an "image" of perfect lives. We go to church with our "church masks" on, telling others that everything is fine, even when our lives might be in turmoil. These "masks" prevent us from living authentic lives in Christian community.

I have often heard people say in recovery that "nobody comes to AA on a winning streak, telling everyone that life is just great." This is true of our guests when they come to The Lamb Center. They are well aware that they are broken by the pain of life. When we join our guests in authentic community, they remind us that we are also broken.

In *Imagine*, DeeAnn Jeremiah brings to life the spirituality of imperfection that is encountered most powerfully at The Lamb Center table. The spirituality of imperfection often follows a pattern of defeat, recognition, redemption and opens the door to this life of abundance.

I am honored to endorse *Imagine*. My dear friend DeeAnn beautifully weaves the relationships and experiences she has encountered with some of our Lamb Center guests. Their willingness to humbly expose the deep wounds of their lives becomes a tapestry that allows us to "imagine" how we can invite the God of Restoration into those wounded places we cover with our "image." God restores the shattered pieces of our past to create a masterpiece. I invite you to enter the lives of some of our Lamb Center guests, as seen through DeeAnn's eyes, and "Imagine" how "I Am" can help you grow in abundant living and authentic Christian community.

Deacon Dave Larrabee,
Director of The Lamb Center,
Fairfax, Virginia

Note from Author

While writing *Imagine*, I talked to countless people from all walks of life. Whenever I explained the premise of this book, with both the idea of covering up our personal hurts with image and the reality that the world is unhinged, everyone resonated with it.

We all thirst for authentic and caring conversations in a more tender environment. We all want to know about our purpose in life. We all want to reveal our aches, doubts, and dreams, but we are afraid to expose our truest selves in such a volatile environment.

Though *Imagine* is an unashamedly Christian book, it exposes the Christian culture and leaves it behind. Here we define *Christian culture* as the "systems, structures, and traditions considered 'Christian' that were built by men, but may *not* be of God."[1] This man-made culture has driven many people away from knowing and connecting with the real God, while it leaves others stuck. Let's just tell the truth!

I write my story from my core belief system, which has changed and grown as I've dug deeper into my own heart. All human beings share a sacred similarity of seeking purpose and joy in life. Perhaps the truths herein will hit a nerve. Whatever our journey up to this point, we all seek a more satisfying and whole life.

As a volunteer at a local homeless day shelter called The Lamb Center, I began to see through other broken people my own brokenness. Their stories reflected my own wounds. As we inspect the lives of the homeless population in *Imagine*, we have the opportunity to see and strip away our own pretenses. Here, maybe we can find the secret to living well. The abundance of life that we all want. We all share humanity and a world together, so let's take a look at commonalities.

Join me to *Imagine* just where we can go in our future and in our world, when we strip away the fake and acknowledge real life, both suffering and hope, within one another.

Introduction

*T*ired of fake, even within the fellowship of believers? Exasperated from getting Bible verse answers when you just need a hug and an "I hear you, friend"? Exhausted from feeling like a salmon swimming upstream in a church world of service that makes it easier to just give up and head downstream?

Most Christians I know are thirsty for wholehearted living, real answers to real problems, and authentic relationships as they follow Jesus in this complicated life. In the book of Acts, we get a sense that believers experienced camaraderie during a difficult time for the new church. Persecution produced communion. Difficulty encouraged sharing the load and helping brothers and sisters along. In our difficult postmodern world with shrinking moral absolutes, and near hostility toward the gospel, the thirst of our soul is for much of the same. We need real community, compassion, and authenticity now, more than ever.

But most of us haven't found it. We have a gnawing emptiness in our souls, even though we might follow God, study our Bibles, and attend church. If we have real problems or bare our honest feelings of doubt, inadequacy, or insecurity, we often find no warmth or understanding. There is little to no tolerance for differing opinions or even genuine conversations. Religious rhetoric does nothing for the deep needs of our soul. So, we avoid the exposure of our own sins, sins committed against us, questions, family conflicts, and generational baggage. Some of us serve until we gain recognition, position, or self-worth (often at the peril of our own health). Others of us cover up our wounds by blending in, scooting in and out of the pew or row of neatly lined-up chairs each Sunday, feeling alone in the "fellowship" of believers. In larger churches, it is easy to remain completely unseen.

We go home and further cover up our deep soul needs with various addictions and affections, not letting anyone see our true selves. Life happens. Depression. A toxic relationship. A divorce. A wayward child. Mental illness. An undiagnosed or lengthy sickness. A lawsuit. Joblessness. An addiction. Suicide of a loved one. Anxiety. A problem with sexual integrity or identity. A newspaper filled with bad and frightening news either over-addressed or unaddressed by our church and community of fellow believers. We may remain largely unknown to others in community. But do *we* even know who we are in the midst of such problems and with so much cover-up? Do we really know who God is if we haven't let Him into the deepest wounds of our hearts? Do we even know our true selves as God intended us to be? Many of us take more time to plan our next vacations or doctors' appointments than to examine who and where we are and where we are really going in life. We rarely contemplate our original design, destiny, and calling God placed deep in our hearts.

Only *I AM*, with our cooperation, can get *in* to the actual heart of the matter, where *real* life begins. Only when we are authentic with ourselves and others can we fully *imagine* all He has for us to be and do.

As I write this introduction, it is Yom Kippur, a sacred day of atonement and one for fasting in the Jewish community of faith. *Atonement* is a theological term about reconciliation between God and man. Although I experienced atonement for my sins when I became a Christian at a young age, I needed a fresh compatibility with God. I wanted His real ways and thoughts to directly intersect with my real life. We were not connecting. My aches and pains had no real life answers. So, while studying the book of Daniel some years ago, I decided to try a fast, just like our Jewish friends do on Yom Kippur. I desperately wanted to hear from God. The questions in my soul weren't being answered in church. They weren't found in the Bible. Friends didn't have the answers.

Oddly, stripping image for me began with a spiritual practice. My soul was starved for answers. If fasting is a common practice for you, it may astound you that I had never tried this discipline. I cut out meat, wine, desserts, and bread (Daniel 1). As I gave God my favorites, I looked at my calendar to make a plan. It seemed nearly biblical and providential that it was exactly forty days until Thanksgiving. And to creatively feed my soul during this season, I decided to do something else I had never done before. I signed up to volunteer at a local homeless shelter.

Ironically, our journey in *Imagine* begins with me, hungry for food and answers, in a homeless day center. Counterintuitively, this "starving" woman with a beautiful home found fullness among the homeless.

The reality is we are all more like the homeless than we care to admit. You'll learn this in each unfolding chapter. Revelation 3:17 says, "You say, 'I am rich; I have acquired wealth and do not need a thing.' But you do not realize that you are wretched, pitiful, poor, blind and naked." Our image only covers up our poverty of spirit to others and maybe even ourselves, but never to God. We are all homeless at heart from time to time. We are naked and pitiful as we try to navigate the unique struggles of life. Those of us who are not literally homeless put up a facade so no one will think less of us. But just *imagine* what we could discover about ourselves underneath the facade.

One can usually tell what might have gone wrong with a homeless person because they are at the end of themselves, with nothing to hide the hurt or reality. They don't care what you think. They are desperate for help. They are hungry for relief. The truth is, that is a much better posture for finding spiritual food and real answers. It is ideal, though not essential, that our authentic and broken spirit is brought to an accepting, slowed-down, loving community steeped in God's love. Just like The Lamb Center. Triage for the poor and poor in spirit. Nonetheless, it turns out God provides clearer answers once we strip away the sound-bite Christian culture of clichés, wherever we are.

Do you live "on the streets" of the community of believers? Are you one of the precious souls who thinks God doesn't care for you anymore because your problems are outside the fences and "in the backwoods" of Christian society? Do you have a hard time even seeing your true heart amid all the clamor and busyness of the noisy streets of opinions and rhetoric? I see you. So does Jesus.

Whether you have found a small group of authentic comrades in the fellowship of believers or you still haven't, come with me to The Lamb Center. Let's discuss *real* life together. Meet some friends who have become homeless. Listen to my story intertwine with theirs. I am sure you can find yourself mixed in there too. The Holy Spirit moves in and around damaged and authentic souls, ours included. At the end of each chapter, I have included "Questions to Ponder" for either personal reflection or small group discussion to facilitate more authenticity.

Jesus came that we "may have *and* enjoy life, and have it in abundance [to the full, till it overflows]" (John 10:10b AMP). Let's begin the journey together. Find my heart in yours. And Jesus' heart in ours. Just *imagine* where He might take us.

Let I AM IN to the heart of the matter.
Strip IMAGE. IMAGINE your destiny with God!

CHAPTER ONE

DeeAnn's Real Life
or <u>First World Problems</u>

*I*magine. Your life as God intended it to be. The great I AM—what were His thoughts and loving plans when He made you? Are you participating with His Spirit in those plans, or are you ignoring the passions, callings, and directions God has placed within you? Have you gotten stuck along the way?

Maybe like I was, you are hung up on God's sovereignty and living life as if you really don't have a choice in the matter. *God will do whatever He wants to do*, you figure. Or maybe you're hung up on image and what being a "good Christian" looks like. Truly, it's hard to imagine the full and abundant plans and purposes God has for you when image, family of origin norms, and societal norms stand in your way.

I'm convinced that digging *in* to your heart and your unique story—the good, bad, and ugly, the guts, and the grit—through the prism of God's redemptive plan, is the way to move forward into your destiny. But first, image must be stripped away. In fact, everything that dares get in your way of knowing all of the true God must be removed.

Cover-up

My journey toward authenticity could have started much earlier. But it didn't. A gnawing emptiness and a cyclical feeling

1

that I had to walk on eggshells in my own home and marriage kept growing. This, in spite of all my efforts to do *all* the right things. I journaled, prayed, and went to church and Bible study, but I couldn't quite put my finger on what was happening to me. I was slowly disappearing. I decided to be brave and approach a long-time Christian mentor whom I admired.

"I've decided to go to a Christian counselor to explore the reason for this awful eggshell-type feeling I'm experiencing at home."

Blank stare. Pause.

"What would people think?" was her only response.

Now, that right there is how toxic relationships and generational sin get cemented into place. The quest for authenticity gets railroaded by Christian culture. Christian culture is defined as "systems, structures and traditions considered 'Christian' that were built by men, but may *not* be of God."[1] One aspect of Christian culture is an overactive concern for image. It may have been passed down by man, but it's not of God.

My mentor put image over wellness, and sadly, I followed her lead. That was the beginning of my years of cover-up in image land. It would be another decade of damage and deeper image build-up before I would seek any help.

Life Goes On

By most measures, I had it all. Success in business. Respect in the community and at church. Beautiful, healthy children. I realized, however, the joyful me was missing, and in its place was a hollowness. My personal church world was running on autopilot. But in the busyness of suburban life and Christian culture, you just keep smiling, keep marching, keep driving, keep carpooling, keep working, keep making dinner, keep pleasing others. And suddenly, whether by an "aha" moment, feeling flat, or getting slapped with the wakeup call of a tragedy like cancer, a car accident, or divorce, you finally get to a point where you ask, How did I get here? What am I doing? Is *this* the plan?

2

I am a huge fan of Jeremiah 29:11: "'For I know the plans I have for you,' declares the Lord, 'plans to prosper you and not to harm you, plans to give you hope and a future.'" Maybe it's because my last name is Jeremiah (how cool is that?), but I think this verse is A-MAZ-ING. So amazing that I had a calligrapher creatively design this verse as a piece of art, which I hung in my great room. This verse has meant much to me during my journey of plot twists and turns.

Maybe you can't fathom what God has in mind for you. Is there really a plan? We rarely continue to the next verses in Jeremiah, which is where we discover how to pursue God's plan. The next verses say, "Then you will call on me and come and pray to me, and I will listen to you. You will seek me and find me when you seek me with all your heart." I read between the lines and hear, "You will find me when you become desperate and go on a soul search and rescue."

The more we unpack our hollowness and explore the depths of our spirit, the closer we get to the crux of the matter. But first we have to slow down or even stop the wheel-like motion of performance and go a few layers below the facade so we can begin to hear from God.

Well, God would bring the most unlikely resource to get me off the hamster wheel of what had become my life.

Stop and Drop

As I pared back the relentless activity, the hamster wheel slowed to a sway. I finally realized I might be playing a part in life that wasn't really mine. After that decade of pursuing image and the perception of correct living, I began to get help. To hell with what other people thought! Therapy. Prayer. Honesty with a few close friends. Though somewhat helpful to me, none of these things brought the breakthrough I sought into my home.

Instead, what finally brought me to my knees, praying to the Savior I'd known for years, was a first world problem in suburbia that just wouldn't get answered by all my performing, or investigating, or trying to cover up the problem: my daughter Joy's eating disorder, anxiety and depression. Among many other problems, this was the dam breaker. My lack of joy and my daughter Joy. Sometimes God has to spell it out.

Get Real

I hunted down therapy, acupuncture, cardiologists, gastroenterologists, medications, and books for my daughter's wellness with moderate success. I also told Joy's youth group leader, my Bible study group, and a few others, who all promised to pray. When it's your kid on the line, these are aggravating baby steps. As a parent, your child's anguish trumps your own. Game on.

Just prior to the surfacing of this problem, my son's public high school began to experience an epidemic of suicide (six in his four years there). Fairfax County has one of the best school systems in the country, for which we moved into our particular neighborhood and entered the rat race of performance for our children's well-being. First world crazy! Realizing the seriousness of depression and the fallout possible from such a competitive environment, I sensed a more systemic problem. Meanwhile, quick emails from church youth leaders inquiring about my daughter's attendance on the mission trip to Romania just about toppled my sanity. Hadn't they listened? An eating disorder was not going to work well in a distant country. Authentic follow up? Nope. Just offers for prayer and more emails wondering why she wasn't attending the fun summer camp coming up. Seriously?

It's as if God said, "Nope, not gonna help you until you get real, DeeAnn. I want to answer DeeAnn's prayers, not the prayers of a suburban Christian with a good girl image to protect." He asked me to get into the grit of me, into the past of me, into the *real* in me before I could get real answers. And like He so lovingly does, He brought a problem I couldn't seem to solve that brought me to the end of my rope. My church world was not helping. Christian culture didn't have the answers.

Don't get me wrong, I know I'm blessed to be one of those kids who grew up in the church and loved most everything about the church. I loved Jesus, and He loved the church, so I did too. Everything from the stained glass windows, to the beautiful dresses and how-do-you-dos in the fellowship hall, to the love and hunger for his Word as I grew in the faith. I have a storage room filled with Bible studies, conference materials, leadership manuals, various versions of Bibles, and hymnals on top of piano sheet music of God's stuff. I'm *that* girl.

It has always been my passion to know Jesus and share Him with others. So my passion for the church and Christendom is paramount. I must say before I go into Christian culture and image: there is goodness and truth at church. But it's not always authentic and real, especially when life gets messy. And *real* life gets *really* messy.

Because my daughter's struggle and my own emotional emptiness were met with shallow answers in Christian culture, I needed fresh perspective. Even though I had known Jesus since childhood, I wanted more. I set out to find something different. I set out on a quest for *real life*.

Oddly, because of the death of a Christian neighbor's son to an accidental heroin overdose after relapsing (another more common first world problem) and the donation we made in his memory, I discovered The Lamb Center, a homeless day shelter in the second richest county in America. Only a few miles from my home, yet worlds away from my comfort zone, I decided to volunteer. Who knew their tagline, "a shelter for the poor and poor in spirit," would deliver all that and more—for *me*!

Out of my regular surroundings, I saw the Holy Spirit move freely through damaged, yet authentic, souls. As I entered into the hurts and needs of others and started being honest about mine, God began to heal my broken spirit. He provided paradigm-shifting answers amid the sound bites of Christian culture filled with smiles and clichés like "Just forgive, forget, and everything will be okay" and "God won't give you more than you can handle."

It took a homeless shelter for me to find the answers God had for me. Had I become homeless? No. But I had become homeless at heart and poor in spirit.

Homelessness and Me

Before volunteering at The Lamb Center, I had seen plenty of homeless folks and was particularly smiley with them during the holiday season, but I virtually ignored them during my twenty-five years of buzzing in and out of the downtown area for our growing business. I had a "Hey, *I'm* working hard over here. You're probably gonna take my hard-earned money for drugs," look the other way at a traffic signal sort of relationship with the homeless. My mom, a deacon for a period of time, told stories about *them,* when they would come to our wealthy church for money or help, but *they* seemed so removed from my reality. So the irony that a homeless day center happens to be a stone's throw from my neighborhood shows how completely blind I was to the stories of others. Well, the donation in lieu of flowers at the young man's funeral turned into a received thank you note and newsletter, which touched something deep inside me. I decided (actually, God led me) to volunteer precious time with this charity.

Who knew this wealth of *real* would bring my joy back like nothing else could? God did! And wouldn't you know, Jeremiah 29:11 is written on a plaque as you enter the building. It's their theme verse too. Was my daughter miraculously healed? No. Not at that time, but she likely will be by the time of this printing. And yes, the suicide plague stopped at our high school, but our country's violent culture of suicide hasn't abated. Even though the culture continues to deteriorate and other problems of life still come, I am walking into the wholeness of life Jesus came to give us (John 10:10). I'm more of the real me, and I know more of the real God. I can see that when you strip away all the nonsense, the Christian resume, the houses, the successes in business, the church world pretense and niceties, the facelifts, the Jesus jewelry and designer bags, you find what is real. Instead of covering up the real, you carefully expose it to others in authentic community and open up every bit of you to Jesus Himself.

Divergent Journey

Although the journey has been long and hard, and often lonely, I am so glad for the *real* He uncovered and is still beautifully uncovering—the whole me pursuing the whole God. I want to learn more about both of us, with freedom, wellness, and authenticity. This has become my battle cry.

You will hear bits and pieces of me throughout the book, so I won't spoil our journey together. It is my goal to encourage you into your story by sharing some of the patterns of family dysfunction (just take a look at the patriarchs of the faith in the Old Testament). As part of God's family, you *are* my family, whether you care to admit it or not. So my story impacts yours and vice versa. We all have something to teach each other. So turn down the noise of this fast-paced world and look in the mirror at your current state of affairs.

No one looks like you or is you. No one can do what you plus God can do. But if you strip off the makeup and the made-up and the cover-up, you can finally see our family resemblance. The good, bad, and the ugly. The homelessness and poverty of our souls (Revelation 3). Temptation, sin, and screwing up what was once a good thing. But also the passion for living. The fullness of life. The unique purpose and calling. The encouragement of the body of Christ. The love of the gospel and the spreading of truth.

God is building His kingdom using frail and sinful saints. He's building His temple with *living* stones (1 Peter 2:4–6), not image-covered ones. You have a part in God's story. Strip away the nonsense. Bring your tired and weary body, your vulnerability, your brokenness, and your pain to the foot of the cross. That is where the real you begins.

My new homeless friends at The Lamb Center, that miraculous place where the Holy Spirit roams freely in others, helped me pick up the mirror and find me. In the coming chapters I will introduce you to them. It is my hope that as you meet our brothers and sisters at The Lamb Center you will meet, in them, more of the real you. Maybe their stories are more like yours than you can imagine.

Have you shaken your fist at God wondering when He will answer your prayer?

Have you been either defined or abused by a parent, a spouse, or someone in your workplace?

Have you had your dreams laughed at or mocked by others?

Have you struggled with forgiving someone who hurt you or even forgiving yourself?

Are you addicted to something, maybe even image?

Well, let's strip image off. Just imagine the abundant life God meant for you—this one sacred and completely unique life. *Yours!*

Questions to Ponder:

1. Reflect on the definition of "Christian culture" in the "Cover-up" section. Discuss some experiences you have had either in your church or Bible study similar to the "blank stare."
2. Does your church or Bible study feel authentic? Describe a time you were nervous to tell the truth about yourself in your church community.
3. Have you ever tried to fit a mold or play a part that wasn't yours? Explain.
4. Explore the word "hollow." Describe when you felt hollow in your Christian journey of faith.

5. Unpack John 10:10. Discuss the schemes of the enemy when it comes to your destiny and God's plan for you. What has been stolen or killed in your life? What does fullness of life look like for you?
6. What are your feelings toward homelessness?
7. Does the idea of homelessness scare you? Challenge you? Or are you unaware of such a problem in your area?
8. What experiences of loss and joy have you had that give you a hint as to where God might be taking you in His plan?
9. How do you relate to being "poor in spirit"?
10. What made you pick up this book? What do you hope to get out of it?

Close by reading Jeremiah 29:11–13. Compare different versions to explore the depth of God's Word.

CHAPTER TWO

Hassan and the Lord's Prayer or <u>Us and Them</u>

*R*adical Islamist. Muslim terrorist. White supremacist. Militant black. Right wing Evangelical. Liberal extremist. Gay activist. Raging feminist.

Labels. Pictures. Don't you get an image in your mind, from your frame of reference, of each of those mentioned? We hear these terms in our everyday lives, progressively sensationalized, pressed into our minds, and we are encouraged to receive them as truth. Social media and the ever-present barrage of the news compete for increasingly outlandish and limiting categories. It perpetuates prejudice and increases anger toward others. Talk about building walls! It is as if by placing people in categories and naming them we can feel safely established and righteous in our opinions. Clearly, we live in a complicated age. No one is immune to the onslaught of name-calling and labeling.

It's a Mixed Bag

Walk with me into The Lamb Center, where this melting pot of labels gets mixed together, then stripped away. All shapes, sizes, cultures, beliefs, and extremes are included among the poor and poor in spirit. Each one comes with his or her own perspective, in need of help. Through the eyes of Christ, rather than labels, we see human beings—bearers of the image of God

(Genesis 1:27). I'll admit, seeing image bearers of God instead of labeling was difficult for me at first. But it became easier after I met Hassan. More on him in a bit.

Having volunteered for only a short while, I noticed on the check-in sheet all kinds of names. Are the poor and homeless all a certain color and creed? Absolutely not. Guests were Latino, black, white, Asian, male, female, gay, straight, and, yes, even transgender. All kinds of people. I live in a transient, multicultural area. As the political landscape changes, our neighbors do too. Recent history has such changes happening more at a rate of every eight years instead of every four, but you get the idea. So, although neighborhoods might stay homogenous, The Lamb Center is more representative of the larger area—the nation's capital.

I had grown accustomed to the variety of life in this area, having friends of different colors, backgrounds, beliefs, sexes, and even sexual preferences. I enjoy it. I especially love the options for eating out and for fascinating discussions. In the Washington, DC, area, politics and controversial topics are not off limits! Folks dive right in for deeper-than-surface cocktail conversation, entertaining a variety of lively opinions and beliefs. It seems nothing is taboo. Yes, some conversations get more volatile as the evening progresses and drinks loosen tongues!

I realize this happens far less in Christian culture. Or in churches. The opinions are more similar, even when they aren't based on biblical truths. A few churches stretch for diverse populations and acceptance in an effort to pride themselves on multiculturalism. Yet how many people would attend a church with a predominant ethnicity different from their own? Thankfully, these trends are changing in some churches, but for the most part, self-segregation by color, creed, politics, and passion occurs. This is unfortunate, as people of all tribes, languages, cultures, and nations were purchased with Christ's blood and will serve our God and reign with Him forever (Revelation 5:9). Christians know this to be true, but often we live as if we would rather put off diversity until the end of time, not be inconvenienced by it right now.

Comical Christian Stereotype

After one of my shifts at The Lamb Center front desk, I decided to attend the morning Bible study at the big wooden table in the center of the great space. I had not yet had the opportunity to lead a study, even though I had checked that box on the volunteer application under what I was willing to do as a "floater," along with laundry (that didn't go well), kitchen (a little better), and leading someone to Christ (hadn't done that yet). Since The Lamb Center had already blasted my normal Christian routine, serving with volunteers from about thirty different churches and many different denominations, I thought I had better listen to the Bible study to see how it was done in this unconventional space. The experience was transformational.

First off, a general stereotype Hollywood developed for most Christians is the free-floating "Jesus freak," who is stupid and out of touch, but really nice. Just think Homer Simpson's neighbor for a picture. My visual was from a sitcom called *The Middle*, which I had watched a few times because it was one of the only decent shows on television to watch with our teen kids. The character's name is Reverend Tim Tom, and he is all the stereotypes portrayed hilariously.

I laughed when I found out the Bible study that day was being led by a guy named Tom. Wait, or was it Tim? I honestly couldn't remember. There was another guy named Tim who also led a Bible study. I got confused, so I secretly referred to Tom as "Reverend Tim Tom," the groovy guitar-playing hippie who ministers to the kids at youth group on *The Middle*. It honestly felt a bit like this to me at The Lamb Center, like the groovy, loving Christians were ministering to the downtrodden. Perhaps we needed some tie-dye t-shirts and longer hair!

In all seriousness, Tom looks nothing like Reverend Tim Tom, but he is kind and warm with a genuine smile and easy manner. Most guests flock to his kindness and his Bible study. After getting to know Tom, I shared my secret classification and name for him. He roared with laughter, saying he absolutely loved that character and was flattered I saw him as such a free spirit!

Already, God had begun his work of stripping me of image — who I thought I was, who I thought others were, and how I thought things should look. Secretly, I'd put Tom in a box, figuring I knew his style and ways. Armed with those preconceived ideas, I labeled this other Christian instead of, by the Spirit of God, looking at his heart. I gladly repented and let the sin fall off me. Yes, we do need to actively participate with God in the process of being real. Little did I know this was just the beginning.

The Table Mix

As always, a mix of volunteers, guests, and staff populated the table. Folks on the perimeter came and went. Noises echoed in the background. It was distracting sometimes, but the study went on. I don't remember what Tom taught that day, but I was blessed by both his leadership and inviting spirit. The discussion was rich and deep.

Tom lived up to some of the stereotype. He asked us all to stand and sing, at which point I thought, "Oh Lord, please don't let it be Kumbaya!" It wasn't, and it went particularly well with the lesson.

As always, we ended the Bible study with open prayer, then closed with the Lord's Prayer (Matthew 6:9–13), which Jesus taught His disciples to pray together. It is prayed at least four times a day at The Lamb Center: before opening, at mid-morning prayer in the chapel, and at the end of both Bible studies. Beautiful.

Mystical Musical Chairs

Just before the prayer, the guest next to me left. As I bowed my head and closed my eyes, I sensed someone else taking the spot as a scent fresh from outside wafted in. Intent on prayer, I continued but noticed my new tablemate was not joining in the prayer. Odd to join late and not participate.

"Amen."

I looked left and saw the new visitor. Handsome, black hair, olive skin, young, tall, misty-eyed, and unsure. I introduced myself, adding, "I haven't met you before. What's your name?" "Hassan," he replied.

Dave, the director of The Lamb Center, was blowing out the candles in the middle of the table. The angel that hung over the wooden cross in the midst of the candles swayed, knocked by Dave's movements. Muted conversations from other participants in the study faded as I focused in on the new guest.

Hassan politely inquired if he could ask a question. I quickly shifted gears from the Bible study, figuring he was going to ask about the assistance programs and services our case managers provided. I casually sized him up to be like many who came to The Lamb Center, just looking for "handouts," because he was clearly not there in time for the Bible study. I assessed those around the table as being there for deeper needs, and in my estimation, he was not in this category. I could not have been more wrong.

Embarrassed as the tears fell freely, he said, "Can you tell me where I could get a copy of that beautiful poem?" Stunned to hear the Lord's Prayer referred to as a poem, I was equally moved by his easy tears and shamed at my presumptuous judgment of him.

"Of course!" I quickly made a move for the staff offices and asked the executive director for access to his computer and printer. Without hesitation or red tape, it was done. I walked out to hand Hassan a copy. He had dried the tears. His posture was both grateful for such a quick answer to his request and a bit embarrassed.

From there, Hassan's story came tumbling out. He'd been sent to The Lamb Center fresh from prison. He still had his belongings in a plastic bag, kept for him during incarceration and presented back to him upon release. He had no idea what we were all about but had a quick referral from the prison chaplain, who had described The Lamb Center as a place to get a good start. While incarcerated, Hassan, a Muslim, though self-described as nonreligious, was introduced to Jesus as the Christ. Flooded with emotion, he described finding a love like he had never known as he learned more about this character he had only known of before as a prophet.

Jesus the Savior

Hassan sat riveted as I explained that Jesus Himself wrote the "poem" he had heard and that it was recorded in the Holy Bible as a prayer, not a poem. It was part of Jesus' Sermon on the Mount, I told him, which demonstrates how His followers are to pray (Matthew 6). Hassan's eyes longed for more. Holy Spirit-led, I asked if he had prayed before or if he had prayed to accept Jesus as the Christ, as his own savior. As he shook his head no, I asked, "Would you like to?"

"Yes!" he said eagerly.

Looking around, I realized that I didn't need to ask anyone to proceed. I didn't need Tom or Dave's help. I was free to follow the Holy Spirit where He was leading. What followed was the gospel narrative, played out amid the simple trappings of The Lamb Center clatter and background noise. Knee to knee, this forgiven sinner fresh from judging another soul (me) sat with a sinner fresh from the prison of death. He recognized the Savior who could remove the stains, pierce the heart, and give a new life. Just like that. Transformed.

I'm embarrassed to say this was the first time I had ever led someone in the "sinner's prayer of salvation" (sample prayer in Appendix). And this, with a convict. Of what he was convicted I have no idea, but it mattered not as I prayed with Hassan, crying too, while he repeated the words I suggested. Then I took the paper I had given him and we read together the Lord's Prayer:

> "Our Father which art in heaven, Hallowed be thy name. Thy kingdom come, Thy will be done on earth as it is in heaven. Give us this day our daily bread. And forgive us our debts, as we forgive our debtors. And lead us not into temptation, but

deliver us from evil: For thine is the kingdom,
and the power, and the glory, for ever. Amen."
(Matthew 6:9-13 KJV)

We opened our eyes to see each other's bright smiles, red
eyes, and tear-stained faces. I stood, and he joined me. Hassan
had to be at least six foot three, but he appeared even larger
in spirit. "Welcome, brother," I said with a giant bear hug. My
newest brother in Christ!

I immediately introduced him as a new brother in Christ
to those who still lingered around the table. And after I gathered my thoughts, I realized this man needed actual physical
help. Just out of prison, he was homeless. No family nearby.
No friends because of the length of his incarceration. I jumped
into volunteer mode, quickly showing him around and speed
talking through all the services provided.

Physical Needs and Appearances

Because I could see the looks of confusion on the faces of
the staff wondering if I had just met a long lost-relative, I gave
the *Reader's Digest* version of all that had just occurred, which
in spiritual terms was monumental.

When Jesus walked the earth, He attended to both spiritual
and physical needs. Neither was overlooked. "I'm starving,"
Hassan admitted. Quickly, I took him to the lunch line, which
was getting long. Then I talked to a case manager, bringing
him up to speed on the story of Hassan. I pointed him out in
the food line, and the case manager assured me he would be
seen and helped.

As I headed off to my world of errands outside The Lamb
Center, I knew this encounter was no accident. None ever are.
Our sovereign God blessed me more than I had ever antici-
pated at my first Lamb Center Bible study. Had I dashed off as
I was tempted to, I would have never had that opportunity. Had
I sized Hassan up by race, gender, stature, and recent classi-
fication (prisoner), I would have never spoken to him. But as

Dave always says as we head over to the table for Bible study, "All are welcome to feast on the Word. Sinners only!" Count me in. Give me more.

All in the Family

Speaking of prejudice, you might remember that old television show, *All in the Family,* that topped the charts of discriminative opinions and outlandish bigotry! Even if our society has progressed in addressing the problem of spoken hatred in public, God has a process to get rid of these judgments from the hearts of His children.

Let's take a look at how all this got started. Many of our preconceived ideas of who people are and how things should be come from the patterns of thought and action (or inaction) in our families of origin and our perspectives on societal norms. It makes a difference where and how we were raised. Everything we've experienced thus far impacts our unique perspectives on nearly everything and everyone.

We all have a core belief system established from our earliest days. It includes how we think about ourselves, about others, the world, and about God. It is influenced by past experiences, culture, faith and values, and current circumstances. Sherry Colley of Rescued for Destiny describes it as looking at the world through distorted or colored lenses—and everyone has his or her own personal prescription!

As I analyzed my preconceived notions and labeling of both Tom and Hassan, I realized none of us are exempt from stereotyping. Before you get too hateful toward a church, our culture, or even yourself, realize those dastardly prejudices and feelings do get shaped in us without our permission. This is brain science. Yes, we can conquer some of these barriers between us and people different from us, but psychological studies prove that regardless of ethnicity, gender, or almost any other group category, all humans tend to relate most to their own perceived groups with higher regard. It is human nature to like people who are like us best. Leonard Mlodinow examines psychological studies of all kinds in his book *How Your Unconscious Mind Rules Your Behavior* (Henri Tajfel, "Experiments in Intergroup Discrimination," *Scientific American* 1970).[1] It is nice to know this is a universal human quality, not just a problem of prejudice in Western culture or in certain people groups.

Yet we know when we receive Jesus, we are a new creation (2 Corinthians 5:17) and we gain the "mind of Christ" (1 Corinthians 2:16). We begin an ongoing transformation (Romans 12:1–2) as we permit God to do His work in us and participate with Him. First, we must be willing to see ourselves as prideful and acknowledge it as sin. Humility begins by seeing ourselves as poor in spirit. Stripping away image and living God's abundant *real* life is about putting everything on the altar before God, even our innermost thoughts.

When we lay everything on the altar before God, He sorts through it all with tender-loving kindness. Don't worry; you get to keep whatever is good! But He *will* point out things that were tacked on by someone or something else that doesn't belong, even something lodged deep in your core belief system. With me, God did this so tenderly and at just the right time.

A perfect prayer of inspection is from Psalm 139:23 which says, "Search me, God, and know my heart; test me and know my anxious thoughts." When we invite God into the heart of the matter, searching even our prejudices, and judgments, He goes in gently.

God loves the spirit of an authentic follower who willingly accepts their real condition, which is "Wretched, miserable, poor, blind and naked" (Revelation 3:17, 1 Peter 5:5). He promises, when we come to Him with our whole selves, He'll put healing salve on our eyes so we may really see (Revelation 3:18).

Eyes Wide Open

As I recollect the day I met Hassan, I realize that had my eyes been wide open, I may not have been so kind. Had I heard his whole story without seeing his true heart need, I may not have engaged him at all. I had already sized up Tom, a white

Christian brother and fellow volunteer. This happened in an instant, and the truth is, had I not been caught off guard, the encounter would not have become a life-changing story for Hassan, or for me. How many more occurrences of grace might occur if my eyes could be closed and my heart completely open to God's leading? How often do we silence the whispers of God with our rational, image-obsessed biases, particularly within the church?

Although my parents were trendsetters coming from the West Coast to the Washington, DC, area in the late 1960s, they seemed somewhat color-blind, truly accepting of those with different backgrounds. When I was a kindergartner, my mom explained the new bussing directives in the county, which would bring more diversity into my classroom. She was so proud that I shrugged it off with an ". . . and" like it would not make much difference to me. One of the reasons they made the move to a more cosmopolitan area, leaving their more homogenous Mennonite upbringing and family, was for the diversity, culture, educational, and job opportunities the Washington, DC, area provided.

That said, I also remember the jockeying and moving to nicer and nicer neighborhoods and learning the word *ostentatious* in fifth grade when my dad wanted us to have a home that looked impressive on the outside, even though it was actually smaller than the more modest-looking home my mom liked. It is so interesting that the status climbing we are encouraged to do with both vocations and homes doesn't match up with the "least of these." Mixed messages for sure.

Inside the church it isn't much better. Although my dad was always proud of the amazing roles my mother had as teacher, mentor, and deacon within the church, he perceived that his position of elder brought a higher level of authority, respect, and honor that was reserved for the successful men in the congregation. How interesting that the work of deacon was much more in line with what Jesus was actually doing while on earth. The deacons at our church are those elected members who are compassionate caregivers, allocating prayer, assistance, and visits for those in situations of crisis, loss, or great need.

Pierced by my own preconceived ideas and quick labeling of people, but beginning to strip off the clear-cut defined roles so firmly in place at my church, I felt the freedom of the Holy Spirit at The Lamb Center. Sometimes structure can hem us into habits that are not godly at all. To think this was the first time I had "led someone to Christ" with this prayer, with decades in a Christ-centered church! With the freedom I was experiencing, I was open to hear God's call to something life-giving. I did not hesitate or feel like I had to run to get a leader who could "surely do this better." What an eye-opener! Where the Spirit of God is, there is freedom (2 Corinthians 3:17). Hassan and I clearly experienced its splendor that day.

Follow Jesus' Example

Even while my eyes were physically closed, I sensed God directing my heart to Hassan. How might your eyes and heart be closed to others from other cultures and creeds? Might God be nudging you to place your inherent labels of others on the altar for Him to inspect and examine? How might God be directing your attention toward others? Are you free enough from perceived authority to hear from God directly? I encourage you to lay your family patterns and perspectives on the altar and press in to I AM and so let Him direct your path to new areas of freedom. Just imagine where God will lead you and what He might have assigned for you each day.

Your heart will be melted into the likeness of Jesus as you, with God, strip away your preconceived ideas about others and listen to what He is saying to your spirit. This is the path to fulfilling your destiny.

Questions to Ponder:

1. What is the predominant ethnicity and religion in your neighborhood? How does this impact you?
2. What is the predominant ethnicity in your church? How does this influence your attitudes?
3. What childhood teachings formed your opinions of outside cultures?
4. Which people group do you have the hardest time understanding?
5. Be honest. Describe the person who would most scare you to be alone with in an alleyway.
6. Discuss frankly how the news impacts your opinions about various cultures.
7. Discuss your favorite story of Jesus breaking racial or cultural boundaries.
8. How might the structures and roles in place at your church or in your circle limit your ability to hear God speak directly to you?
9. Conversely, share an experience when you have been empowered to do or be more than you ever thought possible within your church or circle. Share an experience when your leadership and abilities were highlighted in the church.
10. What kind of labels have you placed on others?
11. What kind of labels have been placed on you?

CHAPTER THREE

Patrick's Wrestling Match
or <u>Wrestle Well</u>

*A*fter the morning prayer, the lights are dimmed and a hush falls over The Lamb Centers' great space. During Bible study, regardless of how many are at the table, Dave, the director, asks everyone to lower their voices in respect for the Word and the discussion.

Some volunteers take their seats, maybe to take a break from serving in the laundry room or the kitchen and get nourished with the Word. Some regular guests are already sitting at the table for a meal or reading the paper and don't feel like moving. They either listen or pretend like they aren't listening. And then there are those who come to The Lamb Center just for the Bible study. Some are former guests who now have housing, but a few are like Patrick, who drives a nice car and has a nice house, but finds this study infinitely more "real" than the ones at his church.

Patrick is an older man who uses a walker. I learned he used to be a college chemistry professor and struggles with an addiction to alcohol. However, what's most distinctive about Patrick is he yells at God. That's right. He yells with frustration that God won't answer his prayers. He yells with frustration that God needs to be louder or closer or more tangible. He yells with frustration that he isn't growing closer to God or becoming more like God. And sometimes, he yells at others who are not being real or who just believe in Jesus and have a carefree attitude, like it's easy. Patrick often says, "Come on. I don't buy that."

Something tells me Patrick may have been led to The Lamb Center for the AA meetings, which are held once a day in the chapel. He seems to know a lot of folks who attend but few of the folks who live on the streets. Like many of us, he has attempted to deal with the symptoms of life's problems without getting to the root of the problems. But while Patrick isn't hunting down the root causes of his anger and self-medicating, he has directed his quest to an all-out wrestling match with God. He is practically turning over tables to get to the bottom of the truth of I AM and to get some of His peace!

Although some people at The Lamb Center think Patrick and his yelling are annoying, I think Patrick is right on target with his transparent relationship with others and his passionate pursuit of God. Passionate and pressing in, instead of pleasant and content with the status quo. Real with Jesus and real with his raw emotions.

Leadings

I met Patrick when I led one of my first Bible studies at The Lamb Center. At this point, I was a substitute facilitator for another dear saint suffering with pancreatic cancer. I knew I had big shoes to fill, as he had been in this time slot for years. I was nervous. Because Patrick was older, I figured he would be a quiet and pleasant addition to the study. Things didn't really go as I expected.

As a substitute Bible study teacher, I didn't have a good idea of how this was supposed to go. All Bible studies I had ever been a part of were planned, with workbooks, notes, a leader, a lecture. This was outside of my Christian standard. Was I supposed to be teaching a lesson or facilitating a discussion?

When I asked Dave if there was any specific Scripture or a book of the Bible the absent leader had been studying or if there was something he would like me to unpack with the group, his answer was, "I'm sure the Holy Spirit will lead you." Thanks . . . I think!

Remember, the Holy Spirit roams free at The Lamb Center. And where the Spirit of God is, there *is* freedom (2 Corinthians 3:17). Because I had no idea what the Holy Spirit was leading me to do, I thought it would be safe to re-teach something I had done before at another Bible study—ahem, when I was prepared with handouts and a colorful cover sheet. So I dug it out and made copies. We had other verses to look up and pretty fonts with the different translations of the Bible. *They will love this!* I said to myself. It was a study of Romans 12:1–2:

> Therefore, I urge you, brothers and sisters, in view of God's mercy, to offer your bodies as a living sacrifice, holy and pleasing to God—this is your true and proper worship. Do not conform to the pattern of this world, but be transformed by the renewing of your mind. Then you will be able to test and approve what God's will is—his good, pleasing and perfect will.

I started. I got a few blank stares. We read the passage out loud.

Patrick yelled, "I don't like the word *sacrifice*. Why did you pick this passage?"

I certainly couldn't get away with, "The Holy Spirit led me to pick this passage." I had to be honest. The Lamb Center requires honesty. "I don't like the word *sacrifice* either, Patrick." I got real with him and managed to work through his fits and spits and calm his angst while also including others in the discussion.

All in all, the lesson went well. I thought incorrectly that I, a student of the Bible for nearly thirty years, would know more than others in attendance. Some of the guests were so knowledgeable. In a church setting, that would have somehow stirred up intimidation or competition. Instead, I was inspired by the rich histories. Gut-wrenching stories. Amazing anecdotes. Heartfelt prayer requests and grateful hearts.

"Someone called back from Veteran Affairs."

"My driver's license came in the mail."

"I got an additional shift."

"I get to go see my daughter this weekend."

"I celebrated a milestone of sobriety."

Wow. That's what I call a transformed mind (Romans 12:2). This is the mind I want to have—one that enables a *real*, grateful, seeing, honest relationship with my Holy God and my brothers and sisters in Christ. I want real, even if it means yelling at God.

I had never heard anyone yell at any of the Bible studies I attended prior to this. However, I do recall the first time I heard a yell in church. A woman yelled "Amen!" *during* a sermon at my proper traditional church. You could almost hear the jaws dropping in righteous indignation! Half of us wanted to know who she was so we could get nerve like her, and the other half wanted to report her to some sort of etiquette containment committee.

Indeed, many who attend the Bible study are startled by Patrick's yelling or are downright irritated by it. Some won't even come to the table when they see he is attending. Because many of our guests struggle with all manner of mental illnesses, PTSD (Post Traumatic Stress Disorder), and trauma-triggered responses, it is a good idea to quickly calm Patrick. But what calms him the most is an honest answer: "I don't understand it fully either, Patrick." A smile. A kind soul who hears and doesn't look away. Someone who sees behind the wounded spirit to a heart that thirsts for righteousness and goodness and answers.

Barbie Doll Bible Study

I'm with Patrick. I'm tired of cover-up. I'm tired of pretty, tidy, Barbie doll Bible study. Subsequent Bible studies at The Lamb Center, thanks to Patrick's lead, have been free-flowing and passionate. They are real. We watch as the Holy Spirit darts us off in many fervent directions, to different Scripture references, to real life struggles, teaching us through each other and our stories. Sometimes God provides comic relief when someone who, indeed, is mentally ill and off their medication says the darndest thing. Or when Alberto, a guest with narcolepsy, falls over snoring. That is *never* the vote of confidence I need! But if I'm real and I'm not impressed with myself or looking for approval, it's just downright comical. Okay, not for him. But come on—remember the story in the Bible when this actually happened to the Apostle Paul (Acts 20:9)? Remember his sermon droned on and a listener fell asleep and out of an open window and died? God restored him to life, but ah, humanity! Same as yesterday and today. A waft of body odor enough to knock you over. An interruption because of a bathroom brawl (I've had those at home with kids sharing bathrooms, haven't you?). It isn't glamorous, but it *is* real. And it has been since the beginning of time.

So I think, in my pretty little life, with a church girl smile, when have I ever yelled at God? When have I *demanded* answers from the throne room? What got my attention enough to say, "That's it! I've had it!" or "When will you ever stinkin' answer this prayer?" When have I been on the narrow edge between hungry faith and desolate disrespect? Let's be real. When have I passionately pursued a prayer and hunted down answers until it hurt?

Well, now that I'm a heck of a lot more real than I used to be, I'll tell you.

Princess Prayers

In her book *The Power of the Praying Wife,* Stormie O'Martian[1] tells how, in her troubled marriage relationship, she prayed specific prayers for her husband and he changed. This, my first prayer book, had me at hello. God's truth, my power as a praying saint, filled with the Holy Spirit and perseverance—sign me up! I wanted more than anything to have a husband who really experienced some joy in life, particularly in our marriage. I had tried everything I had control over, from my physical appearance to a sparkling clean home, to well-mannered children, to healthy meals on the table every night at six o'clock. I had adjusted nearly everything in my power to make him happy. That's a godly wife's job, right? Actually, no. But I about killed myself trying. And trust me, I had prayed. But nothing seemed to be working. So, this book had all the promise of adding biblically inspired prayers, which should ensure success. These were well-designed prayers with Scripture, mapping out every aspect of his manhood I could target. Game on. Since it worked for Stormie, surely it would work for me. So I began praying the Word of God over every aspect of my husband's life. Yahoo! I had finally found my answer. This was all I needed to do.

I am not exaggerating when I tell you this book became *tattered* from constant use. I prayed these prayers faithfully every morning. Each chapter contains an explanation of a certain facet of life and some of Stormie's struggles in that area, followed by a biblically referenced prayer and actual verses for your husband, for his good. It's beautiful. Absolutely brilliantly articulated prayers using Scripture for all aspects of a husband's life—his mind, his work, his sexuality, his attitude, his marriage, you name it. Thirty chapters of topics on every area of his life. It begins with a chapter called "His Wife," and the first line of the prayer section for that chapter is, "Lord, help me to be a good wife." Check. Well, maybe I more resembled a Stepford wife. Some Christian books do not consider the outlier problems of life. It's rarely so cut and dry.

Tattered

When I tell you this book was tattered, I am telling you the binding was broken and the pages were falling out. It was dog-eared and highlighted, with little answers scribbled here and there in the margins and specific additions to the prayer lists written in. More than that, though, *I* was tattered. I was coming unglued. I was grasping with everything in me to make this man I had married completely under the authority of God so I could connect with him. I didn't want him perfect or even close, I just wanted him to want to be closer to me, to be *real* with me. I knew God would keep His end of the deal. I mean, Holy Scripture cannot return void (Isaiah 55:11), so these things had to work, right?

Sometimes in the middle of the night, when I knew my husband was sleeping, I would even hold my hand over him, like a Pentecostal, for a really good covering of prayer. Heck, I had memorized most of the prayers, so I just kept on going to Jesus for this man, who would not seem to unravel his tightly wound hurt. The tenderness I knew had to be inside rarely came out.

The book was my staple during prayer time for at least two years. I was sure prayer was the answer. Heck, an underlined quote in the book was, "Freedom is only a prayer away." Christian culture hogwash. Try telling that to people falsely accused and sitting in prison cells, locked in their situation with no way out. I realized that was me. I was in a prison of sorts, rattling on padlocked bars, getting cold and feeling hopeless. I had done the persevering type of praying and believing. Aware it had not moved my mountains or budged my husband's heart, I finally got to the end of this prayer rope; it almost hung me.

The anger that spouted out of my mouth to God was unlike anything I had ever uttered. Imagine! I was a good girl, a church girl. I stomped into my bedroom, book in hand, slammed the door, and hurled that book as hard as I could against the wall, sealing the fate of its binding for good. I was undone. My shouts at God turned into shaking shoulders, the furious sobs of a broken heart.

"It's not working!"

"I give up, God!"

"Why aren't You answering?"

"Can't You hear me?"

Bible readers know this is *exactly* what David does in the Psalms. We have the privilege of reading his rants. Talk about not worrying, about not having an "I've got it all together" image! Thankfully, we also read his beautiful conclusions that

God does, indeed, hear our cries for help and answers. But today we don't have the full spectrum view of what is going to happen with all those prayers collected in golden bowls (Revelation 5:8).

In what part of Sunday school did I miss the memo that the people in the Bible were living, breathing, stinking, doubting, screaming people who were crying out to God to *listen*? Why did these humans become just like the flannel board figures and remain one-dimensional to me? The living, breathing Word of God had living, breathing people writing it and experiencing angst galore! It's *real*, folks.

Read Hannah's prayer for a son (1 Samuel 1:12–16).

Listen to Ishmael's cry in the desert and God's answer to his mother, Hagar (Genesis 21:17–21).

See the church's prayers for Peter's release from prison (Acts 12).

Look at Asaph's cries for God to listen to his distress (Psalm 77).

See David's prayers for protection from his enemies and their plots of evil (Psalm 64).

These are real people with passionate prayers. At the end of their ropes.

Anger Analysis

Because I can only hear the prayers and not the final answers, I can only give my assessment from this vantage point. What I see in Patrick, as I have come to know him, is his pursuit of God making progress. His prayers are actually being answered. I see the light in his eyes. A kindness in his countenance, not angry at all. I see a reflection of answers in his reality—blooming relationships, great discussions, and positive discourse. He is getting what he is praying for: a closer relationship with God. And as this continues, I can guarantee God will gently pull back his anger to reveal the pain underneath. God will likely use the community at The Lamb Center to do so.

In my situation, I too can see that my prayers from all those years ago are being answered now. Like in the Bible stories of old, the answers are not the ones that were expected. I'm sure a dirty manger (Luke 2) wasn't what people were expecting when they prayed for the return of the long-awaited Messiah. I am certain no one, even at the time, believed a heinous execution (Luke 22:33–49), a bloodbath of Roman scourging, was how God would redeem the world. It certainly wasn't the expected answer.

God's answers have come through my own healing and change. I had to let go of how I thought it was supposed to be in Christianville and embrace my own necessary changes and choices. A shift in the status quo that forces necessary change. This certainly wasn't what I envisioned when I prayed. Coming to the end of my rope in anger was the only way forward. It was giving up, surrendering the idea of the perfection for which I had prayed, the happily-ever-after ending I had hoped would come to pass.

Makeup Remover

So what about you? Are *you* real? Do you shout at God? Have you pressed in for any prayer sustained longer than "Help me on the test tomorrow," or "I need a parking space," or "How about a raise?" If you have, then you know the tiresome prayers of the saints are frustrating business. Can I hear a loud and honest "Amen!"?

Have you prayed over a bruised or strained relationship?
To find a mate?
To get pregnant?
For a wayward son or daughter to return home?
For the salvation of an unsaved spouse?
Maybe like Patrick and like me, for you the frustration is real. The anger is finally showing. Maybe like Patrick, the science professor, and me, the (former) "church girl," things usually don't show up in the packages you expect. Scientific computations

and formulaic prayers don't lead to the expected results in the laboratory of life.

In their deep and brilliant book *Cry of the Soul*, Dan Allender and Tremper Longman III suggest that instead of avoiding all those distasteful and problematic emotions Christians tend to squash, we inspect them to see what truth they hold about what we think about God.

> Ignoring our emotions is turning our back on reality; listening to our emotions ushers us into reality. And reality is where we meet God . . . The presence of disruptive emotions that feel irrational or out of control is not necessarily a sign of disease, sin, or trauma. Instead, it may be the signal that the heart is struggling with God. Therefore, we must view the ups and downs of our emotional life not as a problem to be resolved, but as a cry to be heard.[2]

And God, the great I AM, is listening. He can handle it. He knows what got us into these situations and what brought us to despair. He knows the point at which we will boil over in frustration or blow up with anger. He also knows how to rescue us out of our situations and our shut-down places. But it takes our participation with Him to first strip away any Christian image and strip away our preconceptions about how He will answer—strip away the notion that everything will work out like rainbows and unicorns or that the answers will arrive in some neat little package, with a perfect bow on top of course!

I don't know about you, but I want to be real and live in reality, even if getting to a real solution feels absolutely awful. I want it to be different. Since God is in the real, I want to be too.

So I cried out to God. And He heard my cries for help. Answers came, in cooperation with His Spirit, and they directed me to go *in* and look at my own wounded heart. To weep for myself. To investigate patterns and habits that allowed this problem to take root in my home. To understand people have a choice and may not respond to all God is trying to do to help them. If this were not true, all would be saved and well and there would be perfect peace on earth (2 Peter 3:9).

In answer to my prayers and my heart's longing, God taught me to take action to make some healthy changes for myself instead of focusing on someone else. Not superficial changes to the outside of me or doing more, but making meaningful and real changes on the inside. My *real* and Holy God was with me every step of the way. I never knew freedom could come to my captive heart. But God knew it. He knew precisely the way to bring *real* life, abundant life, life to the full measure (John 10:10). I could start to imagine again, to get a sense of where God was leading me—into the desires, destiny, and calling I AM had planned for me from the beginning of time. I began to feel alive again. *That* was an answer to prayer.

In the Last Analysis

Frustration inside us can often bubble up into anger that flows out of us. Sometimes it is hard to assess if the anger is righteous over injustice or simply a human reaction to a selfish, unmet need. Tremper Longman says, "Injustice is any violation of God's design for life."[3] In that case, it sounds like God is on the side of real, righteous anger about anything standing in the way of intimacy with Him. He doesn't suggest we cover up our desire for more of Him, because He wants us to seek Him with all our hearts, minds, souls, and strength (Deuteronomy 4:29). He doesn't have the Christian culture need to make things look more civilized and dignified.

Take that in for a moment.

Patrick's frustration grows into anger when his desire to understand God and feel His peace doesn't happen quickly enough. He wants more of God. That is righteous anger. Yes, we should be connected with God. And lo and behold, although it doesn't happen as quickly as he would like, the real root of his anger is likely regret over years and years of not knowing

God's beauty and grace. If we even scratched the surface of Patrick's broken home life growing up and the potential reasons he grabbed for medication (booze), we might see an anger God would join in on. It *isn't* as it was supposed to be. That is righteous anger at evil. God agrees.

So our fist-shaking at God is a bit misdirected, but nonetheless safe. As we hold our hurt and inspect it and fall into the heaves of sobs, we join heaven in craving justice. Like the psalmists, we come away seeing that, indeed, the problem is the world gone mad, *not* our merciful Father. He is on our side, inviting us to participate in waging war against evil.

It's an invitation not to cover up the anger, but to *go* there. *Into* the deep. To strip away image and Christian culture prayers (how you think you ought to, or ought not to, talk to God, how you believe He ought to get things done). Instead, weep with God and ask for His hand of direction in what *you* can do to participate in the answer. How might you change the scenario, or how might He change your desire? Now that might make some of you angry with *me*. I hear you. I would have hit me too if I had heard this before I discovered the truth in it.

But you see, God was angry for my pain. He allowed it to be reflected back to me so I could hear from Him. God said to me, "You know, DeeAnn, this isn't working. Stop praying a minute and look at Me, child. Start getting mad at the *problem*. Rage on what isn't right. Start exhibiting the righteous anger that caused Me to flip tables in a church setting. Get to the root of what is going on. Demand better in your home. All you can do, precious one, is change what you will and won't tolerate. *Force change*, daughter of Zion. Get off your knees and wage war against this torment in your home. Get *real*."

What is He saying to you?

Questions to Ponder:

1. Have you ever encountered a rage like Patrick's in a church-type setting? What did you do?
2. Be honest. Have you ever said the Holy Spirit "led you" when you didn't have a clue what to do? Why did you make that claim?
3. When has the Holy Spirit caught you off guard? When did you know He was present and you didn't expect it?
4. Has a truly humble person ever exceeded your expectations and been full of wisdom? What did you learn?
5. What prayer has had you at the end of your rope?
6. When have you experienced rage at an unanswered prayer?
7. Do the Bible stories you know feel real to you or just made-up, like a fairy tale? Give an example of a story you just can't believe would happen and one you can completely see happening even in the here and now.
8. What few people know your deepest longings? Your heartfelt prayers?
9. With what tenacity have you gone to God with your deepest longings and heartfelt prayers? Has He shifted you into specific actions you had to take?
10. What has changed within your heart as your prayer has gone on and on?
11. How might God be asking you to participate in an answer to your prayer?

CHAPTER FOUR

Rose's Rosary or
<u>Performance Prison</u>

*R*ose is one of the older guests at The Lamb Center.
Everyone seems to warm to her and look out for her.
She has a gentle smile, very few teeth, and a warm spirit. Her
face crinkles and her eyes close when she laughs. Her countenance is always upbeat as she asks for her mail. "No news is
good news," she says if there isn't any.

When I learned the details of her past from a national newspaper front page article on "homelessness in the wealthy suburbs," my mouth fell open. First of all, it was a surprise the
plight of the poor and homeless had made the front page of the
newspaper during election season. This was good news. That
I knew each of the three Lamb Center guests of whom the
article spoke was eerily encouraging too. I read quickly to find
out what a reporter's fact finding had dug up about my friends.

When you're a regular volunteer at The Lamb Center, you
know better than to ask, "Hey, how did you become homeless?"
or "What in the heck happened to you?" In fact, a guest who
spoke at the annual Lamb Center banquet said, "It's not like
we grew up dreaming of becoming homeless people someday!
Things just happen." And in the spirit of kindness, you don't go
right to the heart of the matter. That usually happens in safety
and in trust over time.

I found out Rose was eighty-one years old. She was living in her 2002 Ford Focus station wagon with two angel statuettes on her dashboard and all her belongings cluttered in the back seat. I already knew Rose was a devout Catholic—a living, breathing, faithful friend of Jesus. She was incredibly quiet about her faith but never seemed to doubt the goodness of God. Even though her life had been anything but "good." Her husband killed himself in 1972; her eldest daughter was found dead, the cause undetermined, in the woods in nearby Alexandria only two years later; and one of her sons became addicted to drugs and died of an overdose in 2011. Her relationships with her two other children were strained. When I finished reading all of this in the article, I felt I had a better clue of what forces may have deepened the lines on Rose's face. Her tragic life didn't match her cheerful attitude. I wondered what kept her afloat.

Although I'd known Rose's easy smile from working at the front desk on Mondays, the newspaper details made me want to know more of her journey. Thankfully, I got a precious glimpse into her soul at the Bible study at the long wooden table. Her simple story and symbol about being seen and affirmed spoke volumes to my heart. It was the essence of a faithful heart, on an honest path, concerned with God's favor and direction for this journey called life.

More Than Just the Facts

The stories that come around the table two times a day, six days a week, could fill volumes and volumes of books on library shelves and cause an ocean to overflow with tears of heartache. They are much more passionate than the facts of a newspaper. I'm relatively new at The Lamb Center, a volunteer for only a few years. Some volunteers span decades. Imagine the countless stories they have heard. I am blown away that these dear people, the volunteers and the homeless, still stand upright after the horrors of injustice, tragedy, and discouragement. God's heart must break again and again. Why don't our hearts break for fellow human beings? The nerve of me glibly saying, "How are you today?" or "Can you believe how cold it is today?" Usually those on the other end of these brief exchanges politely agree instead of saying, "Child, you have *no* idea!" Grace abounds.

An Invitation to the Table

Rose timidly approached the table to sit down for a bite to eat. I overzealously asked her if she was joining the Bible study I was about to lead.

She shrugged. "Oh, I don't know."

I shamelessly begged her to stay.

With a sparkle in her eye she said, "Only if I can sit by you!"

As she sat down, I patted her knee under the table, and she grabbed my hand to hold it as we prayed. I knew her presence would not only add to the warmth of the group, but it would help me really *see* Rose. And myself reflected in her eyes.

I can't remember exactly what question I posed to the group to facilitate a discussion, but I do remember it drew out deep waters and rich answers wrapped in simple stories. The question had to do with a way you felt special or recognized or loved when you didn't expect it. I asked it simply to draw out those who rarely shared. It was meant to stump the "smarty pants" folks because they had to reflect on themselves instead of the words on the pages of Scripture. It didn't have religious overtones; it was more like a get-to-know-you type of question.

Rose, sweet catholic girl that she is, raised her hand. I picked her and her eyes danced, just like they must have when she was a girl in her story. She described her strict catholic school upbringing. Vividly we could see her timid little girl self, all of seven years old, sitting in her uniform jumper, her legs crossed at the ankles under the desk, face downward to avoid attention.

Sister Martha was getting ready for classroom announcements, and Rose was minding her business, listening but not looking the teacher directly in the eye. Lacking confidence. Feeling invisible. She waited patiently, fiddling with her pencil.

Students were called forward for various awards. One boy came forward for perfect attendance. Another girl won a spelling award. Then it came time to give the award to the student who most resembled the attitude of Christ in kindness shown to others. The other teachers, mostly other nuns, had come to a decision and were very glad to give the award to . . . Rose! Her name was called aloud. Never popular or a standout, Rose was stunned. Flabbergasted. She said she didn't even think the nun knew her name, as she was rarely called on in class.

She looked up in surprise. Sister Martha invited her up in front of the whole third grade class. Gawks and snickers came as Rose bravely left her seat for the front of the room for an accolade, instead of a spanking. To her sheer delight, she was presented with a small velveteen box. A gift. As the sister opened the box, Rose's hands flew to her gaping mouth. It was a crystal rosary! Rose had won the award for resembling the attitude of Christ in her kindness to others. For her, though, it was the "being seen" award.

Rose was so excited to be seen and affirmed by the nuns. With a gleam in her eye, Rose went on to tell us she had kept the rosary, in its original box, for all these years. At eighty-one years old, living in a car, with few earthly possessions, this rosary was more precious to her than gold.

It made me think how important it is to be seen and affirmed. I know that even when no one else sees, God sees me. And God sees you too. He sees every heart and knows every intention (Psalm 11:4). He sees all pain, knows every sorrow, and knows when we are unjustly treated. Your heart's deepest desires and original passions, placed there by God, along with your destiny for which He created you, are indeed known and seen by God, the great I AM.

The God Who Sees
"The God who sees." Hagar first coined the phrase in Scripture. Remember, she was the maid of Sarai, who was the wife of the famous Abram. Sarai had cooked up a scheme

to make God's promises all work out well by taking matters into her own hands and having Abram sleep with her Egyptian maid. It was fairly common in those days, but really? These Old Testament guys had quite the life. Anyway, through this union, Hagar became pregnant with Ishmael, who is literally the father of the Arab nations and Islam. Once she was pregnant, Hagar treated Sarai with contempt, and in turn Sarai treated her very harshly. Hagar fled into the desert with Ishmael (Genesis 16). She would rather die with her son in the desert than continue in the abuse of this contrived and manipulative system. I hear you, Hagar. God sees you, Hagar.

God, as He so tenderly does, came to Hagar, and the Angel of the Lord asked her a question. "Where have you come from and where are you going?" (Genesis 16:8).

This is a deep question. Multilayered and direct. Maybe in a desert environment it would be easier to answer than in our noisy society.

Most of the time in Scripture we see God or His messengers *tell* people what is going to happen. But to Hagar, He *asked* the million dollar question! What a privilege to answer God.

I sensed God was asking me too. "DeeAnn, where have you come from and where are you going? I see you, child of Mine."

Rose-colored Glasses

Rose was seen and affirmed by the authorities, the nuns, in her life. Though she wasn't seeking praise, my case was different. I was nearly obsessed with being affirmed by my parents and other people of prestige. *I* wanted a prize! Rose's affirmation by the nuns reminded me of the way I lived to be applauded by others. It became more important to me than anything else. Even more important than being seen and adored by God. And this realization triggered something deep in me.

I realized I needed to ask *myself* some hard questions. Where am I? Where am I going? How did I *get* where I am? Is this what *I* dreamed of? Didn't I AM already have where I was going worked out? The search for real answers took digging *in,* to a place I had put away a long time ago. Digging in to the heart of the matter. Ouch. I didn't expect it to hurt so much.

At first, I found more questions than answers. If I was doing all the right things and being the good girl, why was my heart breaking in loneliness inside my own well-appointed home? Why was there no laughter in my heart, no sparkle in my eyes? While there were no prizes from nuns or pastors like Rose had received and no brownie points for church attendance or godliness lined up on my trophy shelf, I did have flattery for all I had done. I was performing beautifully and winning accolades from my parents, friends, and fellow parishioners. But my shoulders ached from the doing. From hypervigilance. My heart shriveled from personal image focus, which wasn't leading me to my true self at all.

The Old College Try

My mom was a third grade teacher for what seemed like centuries. It was her favorite grade. She said the kids had a thirst to learn, were motivated to please, and hadn't yet been hardened by the ways of the world. Her perfect mode of positive reinforcement in the classroom worked miracles with these little ones. It is a good classroom strategy for sure, but I'm not so sure just applauding the "staying in the lines" was best for a beloved daughter, especially when that tactic seemed to go on through college and beyond.

These thoughts and memories helped me see Rose with clearer eyes. And helped me see *me* with clearer eyes. My whole life, I had been like Rose, always doing right. Top of the class. Kind to others. Being the best I could be. Always thinking about others instead of myself to make sure everyone thought well of me. Believing it was more important what people thought I was than what I actually was. Image. That was how I lived. And it manifested clearly in my college years.

I was magna cum laude—all about the performance and looking good at my large public university. I gave out way too much of my heart in a lush of lovely *real*. Joyfully, I shared all my feelings and thoughts with everyone, especially my parents. It didn't occur to me that they could be used against me. I respected other people's opinions just a little too much. I was so trusting and needy, begging for my parents' approval every step of the way. Even the distance while studying abroad in London didn't change my need for affirmation. Approval was my drug of choice. I don't think I even tried beer until my second semester junior year and it was at a pub discussing an assignment with a British professor! And being "damned by faint praise" was the worst. It was my Molotov cocktail. Enough to turn the tides of any decision. It killed my passions, my choices, my joyful heart. The result of my addiction to affirmation was that I made significant choices that altered my destiny, stabbed my own heart. Driven by my need for approval, the suggestions of my parents and a pastor would trump even God Himself giving me a directive.

When I was a senior, I fell in love with a down-to-earth and tender man—the "one" whom I told Mom all about. It was going in the direction most loving relationships between people at that age go, toward the altar. But my mom wanted something "better" for me. She and the pastor had picked a different man who was well-connected, older, and more polished than the man I loved. My mind and spirit were heavy with a tug-of-war type of pain. I grappled with what they thought was best for me and what my heart was clinging to; the two concepts were at odds because of my need to have all my choices affirmed.

Meanwhile, I was finishing up my final classes, and part of that was a required interview with a communications professor. After our meeting, the professor—a Christian, unbeknownst to me—invited me to pray. He said God was "leading" him to pray with me. I was stunned. How random. I'd heard about miraculous prayer interventions at critical junctures in books and in movies, but this was my life. I agreed, because I always said yes to authority, especially godly authority.

He didn't know me personally. He didn't know my situation. But he prayed what God led him to pray. It was prophetic, Scripture including Psalm 19 about the sky declaring the glory of God. And a passage from Isaiah. After praying with the professor, the takeaway from God was that my heart was on the right track with the man I loved. My heart soared. Burden lifted. "You are doing right, DeeAnn! You *are* following My heart and the destiny I planned for you." Imagine!

And then, I doubted. I called my mom for affirmation, hoping she would hear this as good news. Instead, she asked about this professor, his "theological resume" and background. Because the message that came from God in this supernatural and unique way altered her expectations for me and my future, she dismissed the odd occurrence. And like a good school teacher does, she quickly changed the subject to something more positive, like grades and graduation. I was devastated.

That night on a teary walk across the lawn of the quad, under the sky so beautifully described in Psalm 19, I asked God for a sign of confirmation of the earlier prophetic word (after He had already shown up so strong). And in that moment, God *shouted* His previous message with two blazing stars shooting across the landscape. This had never happened to me before. And hasn't since.

Once you refuse to hear the voice of God in a certain way, I'm convinced He chooses to speak in different ways so He can be heard . . . if we will listen. And when we won't, sometimes God goes silent. He lets our choices be the answer. And some choices hurt to make.

In that dramatic moment on the quad lawn, I chose to ignore His direction, opting for my parents' ideas instead. I thought doing all my parents and pastor suggested and following God were one and the same. My parents were godly, and I was following them, therefore I was doing what was godly. To me, it was that simple.

And let's face it, this supernatural occurrence didn't fit the expectations of our family church theology or our image of how prayers get answered. Heck, if the professor spoke in tongues, without an interpretation, my parents probably would have pulled me from the university! Not enough "religious correctness" for Mom's nod of approval. And honestly, that mattered more to me than whatever God had to say.

I altered my course. It was all on me and my choices. I wanted the paved way that was the church world. It's easier to have your family all in agreement. Christian culture is a bit like the paved sidewalks around the university quad lawn. Tidy. Immaculate. However, no free-thinking student uses them! They all do the Xs and zigzags across the dew-covered lawn, dodging co-eds throwing Frisbees, or lovers kissing on a rock, or a professor having class outdoors in the middle of the quad on a sunny Friday afternoon.

But I wasn't one of those students. I left the beauty of my divine intervention on the lawn of the quad and instead retreated to the pavement. I said goodbye to my "true love" and decided to walk the path others deemed best for me—the *he already has a reliable job and a predictable future* type of path. My mother's pick had pedigree connections in my prominent hometown, strong ties with pastors, the church, and family friends. That plus his good looks, his age-up knowledge of most topics and places, and his ability to afford nicer dates made this all quite easy. However, his heart was lukewarm to free-flowing words, and the lush of real, and discovering new places, and coloring outside the lines. He was rather amused by my simple views and naiveté, which just made me try harder to win the favor of the "best" who was picked out for me.

Stay in line. Stars and brownie points. Accolades in the northern Virginia land of goodness. I crucified my heart. I blocked my ears to God's instruction. I began to travel into image land. Indeed, I would win the approval of many, the envy of others, and the admiration of those after me. But if they could only see through the facade—and ask what God asks us:

Where *are* you, DeeAnn? Where are you going? Are you listening to the heartbeat of Me and to what I put in your heart?

The Rosary

Fast forward to fifty years of my life. The Rosary, five decades of mystery. Beads on a string—a garden of prayers. Remembering the life of Christ. Thinking of precious Mary, mother of Jesus; precious Rose; Precious DeeAnn. Pure, simple women, seen by God. Favored ladies, yet bearers of different kinds of death. Birth, then death to the Savior of the world, for Mary. Death in life for Rose. Death of real and a true love for me.

Mary was seen and chosen by God. She was obedient to a path she didn't choose, but through her obedience the world was altered and saved. Her reputation was sullied, even though the words of Scripture will forever call her "highly favored lady" (Luke 1:28).

Rose was seen by God, yet surrounded by death. She brings simplicity and hope to the hopeless. She still sparkles and believes in God's goodness and in the angels who protect her.

DeeAnn was seen and heard by God. Prayers counted in golden bowls (Revelation 5:8). A garden of prayers. Tears recorded on God's scroll (Psalm 56:8). A much more simplistic sovereignty of lineage than Mary. Nowhere near the suffering and pierced heart of Mary. Nowhere near the emotional death blows Rose endured.

But grief nevertheless that eventually led to healing my approval-seeking habits. Promise and restoration in the generation ahead. Extraordinary children who are the perfect chemistry of me and my husband. Thy will be done. Despite walking a path others had designed for me, despising my own sacred heart and God's direction, His sovereignty overrode it all. He redeems and restores what is lost and broken. God works it all together for our good and His glory (Romans 8:28). Because of Rose, I was able to work through those hurts from years ago. I could forgive myself for needing approval of people more than

God. I accepted His forgiveness and let it seep into old college wounds. I let Him into that deep part of my heart for restoration.

I now play my own part in my story. I listen and respond to God's voice. I look for His approval. I keep my eyes open to supernatural occurrences, which now happen more frequently. I know He always sees me and hears my prayers. The rosary of life always begins and ends with the cross of Christ. Beauty and renewal often come through anguish and sorrow.

> Our Father, who art in Heaven, Hallowed be thy name. Thy kingdom come Thy will be done, on earth as it is in heaven.

> Glory be to the Father, and to the Son, and to the Holy Ghost. Amen.

Where Are You?

In this busy world filled with so much noise and idle chatter, take time to investigate where you are in life. In the bustle of plans and checklists, bills and babies, take some time to self-assess.

Brother or sister, where are *you*? How did you get where you are? When did you meet the Master planner? Are you on His course?

What pain has come from your choices? What good has come from your obedience? Have you been following Him, following your whims, or following a path that isn't yours at all? Did your path have an unexpected turn you couldn't control?

What were your plans? How have they been altered? Are you staying true to your story and God's approval?

Where Are You Going?

Is someone, anyone, more important than God in your life? To whom do you listen? How does your heart respond?

Destiny depends on the journey. It winds and weaves through desires and the choices we make. Through suffering and altered plans.

We all have a story to tell, so be your truest self, seeking the true God (not others' approval). Take some time to answer Him directly. It is not too late. Treasure the pleasure of being seen and known by God. It's a gift in a velveteen box, kept safe just for you. He longs to hear your answer. He longs to give you your heart's desire as you passionately follow His lead (Psalm 37:4). Wherever you've been, and wherever you are . . . where you are going is up ahead. The great I AM would love to imagine it with you.

Questions to Ponder:

1. What was your reaction to Rose's story?
2. Describe the face of an older person you adore. What characteristics bless your soul?
3. When have you been seen and noticed when you didn't expect it? Do you have a childhood story about being recognized? Share it.
4. How have others' assessments of you shaped who you are today? Are you addicted to affirmation?
5. What was your college or young adult experience? Did you end up becoming more like yourself or more like someone else?
6. If you have experienced a "divine intervention" or supernatural event, share it. How did the experience change your view of God?
7. How have significant choices in your past altered your current reality?
8. Where are you?
9. Where are you going?

CHAPTER FIVE

*"F***ing Queer"* or <u>**Renamed**</u>

*M*onday mornings come early for most people. But for those living on the streets without shelter, Mondays can't come soon enough. Day shelters like The Lamb Center are usually closed on Sundays. Many who are homeless have no predictable shelter, covering, food, or bathroom. With weather conditions added to the mix, the homeless anxiously await the open door at 8:00 a.m. As a volunteer, it makes Mondays a bit of a "you never know what you're gonna get" at The Lamb Center.

During the winter months, local churches surrounding The Lamb Center open their doors for a week at a time so the local homeless can sleep in fellowship halls and corridors instead of outdoors, where they are at risk of hypothermia. Overnight shelters are distant, hard to get to, and generally packed like sardines. Although the kindness and practicality of the "hypo-thermia prevention" campaign is amazing, it is a long winter for the guests. Being closed in tightly, with no personal space, heightens frustration, which contributes to disagreements, fights, and even arrests. It's a stressful season. Some of those hypothermia-related deaths in wealthier counties have little to do with available beds in shelters and more to do with those homeless who prefer the peace of the cold outdoors to the stress from closeness with irritable and often volatile people.

Weather reports might inconvenience the rest of us by dis-rupting our plans to get out of town for a ski trip, our commutes to work, or our heating bills, but the weather reports completely paralyze those who have mental illnesses, physical disabilities, no housing, and no transportation. Even those who live in their cars are often low on fuel. They frequently hunt for secret places to park and sleep, as the police and store owners are ever nudging them out of the public view. Understandable, but also incredibly agitating. Regardless of whatever caused an individual's homelessness, these are fellow human beings. Our American culture seems to have more compassion for a dog left in a cold car or baby seals in the arctic than the homeless human beings on the street.

A Classic and Real Concierge

This sets the stage for one particularly cold winter day, a Monday morning, when tensions were already high with guests anxious to get inside, warm up, and get something to eat. Many needed a hot shower before work or help from case managers or local social workers regarding housing assistance from Fairfax County.

On the drive in, I prayed that I would be quick to remember names and faces as I check in each guest. That I would be warm-hearted and cheery as I welcomed the guests at my post at the check-in desk, even if I didn't wake up enough in time to join the staff and volunteers in the chapel for our fifteen minutes of prayer before the doors open to the public.

Funny. My husband and I expect all the employees of our concierge business, called Classic Concierge, to be on the job a little earlier than their shifts begin so they will be prepared. Our employees are those gracious and friendly people in building lobbies who greet tenants, residents, and guests. Our mission statement says we will be kind and courteous to *everyone* entering the doors.

We also promise to help building managers maintain a nicer ambience in their lobbies by keeping out vagrants (homeless people). Our business clients enter their workplace environment, a glorious marble lobby, where they are greeted by a professionally dressed concierge who is paid to honor their presence and remember their names. Back in the day, as a struggling entrepreneur, I worked at the front desk at one of those fancy locations (our very first contract) while writing our company's first training manual about the importance of early arrival and learning names and faces. Now, all these years later, I am volunteering at the front desk of The Lamb Center. God does have a sense of humor when it comes to the places He takes us to get our *real* on. Back to the future—and in dress-down mode. Ha! I'm the concierge for The Lamb Center!

Anyway, I hadn't had my morning cups of coffee and my brain needed to start functioning. I was finding showing up at The Lamb Center particularly hard that morning, that is, until I remembered the guests and saw their faces in my mind. How dare I complain about having cold feet on my bathroom floor and not being able to find my slippers? Sheesh. It's hard to complain for long about such first world problems when someone you now know has been cold all night.

What's Your Name?

As the morning unfolded, I did my best with names and faces and felt proud of myself for being so dang on the ball so early. Besides names and faces, though, everyone who walks in the door has baggage, both the stuff hauled behind them in roller suitcases or carried in tote bags and the stuff of their past—what got them to the place of poverty in the first place. I have some too. Don't we all?

I had just finished checking in the first wave of guests who had been waiting in the parking lot for the door to open. A slight pause and a moment to check mail for a few guests, answer questions, and take a few calls. Then he came in.

I had never seen him before. He was a shorter man with a blended Asian ethnicity and skin leathery from living on the street. His thin frame was evident by the belt cinching his baggy jeans, and his cheeks were gaunt from lack of food and perhaps lack of teeth. Because of the set of his jaw, I sensed tension.

49

I said, "Last name, sir."

He mumbled. And with his mumble I realized that his lack of teeth and possible language barrier were going to make communication difficult.

Hesitantly, I asked again.

He mumbled louder.

I still didn't understand. To ease the awkwardness, I offered a pen and paper and asked him to jot down his name so I could get it right on the roster.

Well, that was *it!* Undone and furious, he yelled at the top of his lungs, "'F***ING QUEER' WHAT THEY CALL ME!"

Now, a firm rule at The Lamb Center is absolutely no swearing, and raised voices are prohibited. Initially, I thought it was rather legalistic. I mean, if I was on the street and frustrated as hell with my situation, I might feel like throwing out an "F-bomb" from time to time. I know that doesn't match up with my personality or a Christian organization, but seriously, this sh** is awful. No swearing? Come on.

The purpose of the rule became evident to me, though, when on an earlier occasion a guest lost it and yelled an obscenity about the state of our country and the news. She was near the front desk, and it was not directed at anyone, but the ricochet of pandemonium that spread throughout The Lamb Center was like the outcome of freaking out an entire den of nervous cats. This rule is, indeed, brilliant and necessary. It prevents a multitude of problems. With many of our veterans and other guests struggling with PTSD, one outburst or loud sound sends a host of other guests over the edge to panic and chaos.

Following the launch of fury from this new man, I immediately moved to pacify him, worried he would be asked to leave. My natural instinct of shock and fear was quickly replaced by calm and compassion. My heart broke for him instead of retracting in horror or falling into "rule-breaker justice" mode. The man marched off toward the laundry area, completely ignoring the process of checking in. I sat there in stunned silence and glanced over to the breakfast eaters and coffee sippers and showed a calm "I got this. No worries. All peace!" to them, as if by harnessing my own peace they too would stay calm. Praise God they did. Knowing that again the guest would have to give his name at the laundry counter so they could track the loads of wash, I nervously intercommed The Lamb Center's director, Dave, to come out and see me.

Dave is the kindest and calmest man under pressure I have ever met. He is simply never ruffled. I could tell the guests were significantly more calm once he stepped out into the open community room. His presence is like the Holy Spirit; everyone is instantly at peace when he is around.

"Is everything alright?" he asked.

I reassured him everything was fine, I just needed his advice.

I quietly explained to Dave, pointing with eye movements toward the man, what had just taken place. As we spoke, the laundry folks, who had heard the tirade, took his laundry, no questions asked. His anger kept everyone at arm's length. He was a master at making a prison of loneliness for himself. Tragic.

"I have an idea," Dave said.

He wrote on a scrap of paper *Good Man*. Then, smiling and confident, he walked over and handed it to the man over by the laundry area, saying, "We will call you this."

The man nearly bit Dave's head off, exploding again. "ONLY ONE GOOD MAN!"

I gotta say, right on, brother. I hear that. No swearing, and biblically accurate. He was a truth teller for sure.

Dave returned rather timidly to the front desk. "*That* didn't work!"

No kidding. Brainstorming again, I suggested, "How about Forgiven Man?" My logic was, if he knew about Jesus' goodness, he could access forgiveness. This might be a beginning. Maybe we would have a breakthrough.

Dave and I decided that, rather than approach "Forgiven Man" again for his stamp of approval, we would kindly name him ourselves. With that settled, Dave walked back to his office to enter the new name on the computer roster.

At 11:00 a.m., my shift was over, and Margaret, a longtime volunteer, dutifully relieved me at the front desk. As usual, we exchanged pleasantries, and I filled her in on what had transpired during the morning, including, and especially, the experience with our new guest. I suggested leaving him to himself. No need for another cheery volunteer to set off the ticking time bomb of "Forgiven Man." Quite honestly, I just didn't want to get him in trouble with The Lamb Center rules. Strangely, I felt drawn to his story. I took it with me out into my world to ponder. I identified with his hostility just a little too much.

It's from SOMEwhere

Years earlier, as I was working through a ladies Bible study on the fruit of the Spirit (Galatians 5:22–23), I heard some sage advice from Beth Moore: "If you have a feeling that pops up out of nowhere, it's from *some*where!"[1] It's best to stop. Be present. Invite the Holy Spirit to explore this part of you and to illuminate what just happened. Really good advice that I would be able to apply sooner than I realized.

One evening during this same season of life, I was working on my computer and behind schedule with dinner preparation. My husband, from the next room, yelled out a comment I had heard countless times in my marriage. It wasn't anything new or particularly mean, but more a dismissive, snarky comment while he relaxed in front of the television. "Is dinner going to be *ready* at six?"

I'd recently started seeing a counselor at our church to investigate why my usually joyful spirit was feeling less than real. I parked a good two blocks away and wore dark glasses so no one would notice me. After just one session, I became much more aware of my surroundings. I started listening differently. And when I listened to those familiar words and tone of my husband that day, they finally hit a nerve.

I walked into the bathroom, put my hands on the counter, and looked deeply in the mirror. My perky smile was completely gone, and a scowl furrowed my eyebrows. My temples were pulsing, and I mouthed what looked like a scream but was completely silent: "I HATE HIM!" I was shaking with pure, unadulterated fury.

Now, I don't have a darling Southern accent like Beth Moore, but I could hear her drawl from the video: "Holy Spirit, wha-t was THA-T?!" (There should be approximately three drawn-out syllables for *what* and *that*.)

In an instant, the Holy Spirit beamed a word to me I had not articulated because of my frenetic activity and hypervigilance. It was P-A-I-N. Deep-seated hurt. I was the walking wounded. I had been going along, singing a song, when BAM. There it was. It was ugly.

Daughters of Presbyterians, who were formerly Mennonites, do not have a mean bone in their bodies. They certainly *never* hate anyone. In fact, I believe *hate* was on the "bad word list" my mother had, along with the words *bored* and *shut up*. And we never ever ever fight back. We're pacifists. We turn the other cheek and do kind deeds to anyone who hurts us. We faithfully explain away any negativity by considering the other person's day, or plight, or issue. We never think about our own feelings. And if we do, and they are bad, they *must* be dismissed.

If you were raised like me, you think, *What would Jesus do?* The kind-hearted Jesus with free-flowing hair comes to mind—a Jesus swinging children around in fields, a few wildflowers blowing in the wind. He smiles and shares a poem or a lovely parable of some type, which successfully distracts everyone from pain. You never try to find out why you would have such a terrible reaction. It must be your sinful nature popping through to the surface. Bury it quickly, put your smile of the love of God back on your face, and get out there to your family. Work hard to make sure dinner is on the table in time, for goodness' sake. You wouldn't want to make your husband more sour than he already is.

No More

Because that season of counseling at the church helped me identify my problem at home, I did further research secretly in a public library, scouring books that introduced me to profound insight and health. Yes, hurt people hurt people. Those who have been damaged damage and hurt others. I learned about boundaries. And what forgiveness looks like. Not forgetting, but remembering well and changing the patterns. You can only change yourself. You are the only person over whom you have control.

But most importantly, anger *is* unresolved hurt.

My heart bled for me.

It bled for my wounded, wounding husband.

It bled for my marriage.

It bled for my children.

It bled for the homeless.

It bled for Forgiven Man.

I hear you. I see you, behind your screaming, aching heart.

I also learned that anyone who defines you in any negative way, even in a "just joking" way, is abusive. It's called emotional abuse. Sometimes it comes out as verbal abuse, but in church world, the words are not usually coarse enough to alarm us or others. The words are subtle, smart, and usually couched with the biblical doctrine of submission and self righteousness. It's an age-old strategy from the serpent in Genesis, from the pit of hell: know the truth better than the victim and twist it ever so cleverly to leave confusion and delusion in the path. "You" statements are defining, controlling, and can be used by manipulative abusers.

"You always . . ."

"You never . . ."

"You love this . . ."

"You are that . . ."

"You specifically said this . . ."

"You" anything.

Nope. My spirit will *not* be broken.

I am me. I decide what I like and what I feel, and I am free to express those things to your preconceived notions and controlling tongue. I will not be fooled, even when no swear words are used. *No more!*

Reflections

Precious man. Forgiven Man. What happened to you? The loud swear word preceding this awful, defining name you've been called awakens me to what I know: Forgiven Man has been *severely* abused. And his spirit broken. Who told you what you were? Who was abusing you? Don't believe those lies. Break that agreement with the enemy of your soul. You are you. Strip away this lie. Find yourself. Before everyone is running from you. Before your twisted mind is in ruins. Perhaps in the quiet setting of The Lamb Center with its kind rules you can rest awhile. Sit with the Holy Spirit and dig down to find the "Where did that come from?" "How did I become "F***ing Queer?"

What covers my real name—the real me? Who does GOD, the great I AM, say I am?

Friend, who are you? Who do you say you are? Who have others said you are? Have you listened to our defining culture? And not just the heinous television culture or the culture of nonstop abusive language—"Idiot," "Loser," "Slut"—on social media. Think also of the culture within your home. Dig *in* and explore your environment for any hint of emotional abuse, characterized by behaviors which insult, isolate, humiliate, degrade, control, or manipulate another person. Inevitably the actions make you feel like less of the person you are meant to be.

Verbal abuse is easier to spot because it defines the other person negatively. It has become so common in our hostile culture we tend to dismiss it, but human beings are sacred, made in the image of our most holy God. *You* are sacred.

In my situation, I had to change my posture, shift boundaries, and plug my ears to the Christian culture of easy fixes. Life is a process. That's why I pressed in to God for *more!* His very Spirit led me to strip off the Christian image of "everything is okay" and instead identify and deal with the verbal and emotional abuse in my life, past and present. Stuff people slapped on me and I received as truth. Such language affects our thinking and perspective; it affects our behavior. It causes us to ask, "Why do the same things keep happening to me?" We usually repeat the same patterns over and over in our thematic lives. It's what humans do. But I want life to the full. I want what God wants for me. I bet you do too.

God promises that He has a new name for us—*His* name. We are *His* children. ". . . I have called you by your name. I have surnamed you, though you have not known Me" (Isaiah 45:4b).

So, welcome to The Lamb Center! God's Lamb Center. His triage unit. What is *your* name?

I see here on the updated roster under the Fs we have *Forgiven Man :)*. I know Dave put the smiley face there just for me!

Questions to Ponder:

1. Have you ever encountered a person like Forgiven Man? What are some of your experiences with the mentally ill?

2. How would you have handled the situation with this hostile man?

3. Remembering names and faces is difficult for some. Think of a time when someone remembered your name when you didn't expect it. How did it make you feel?

4. Carefully think through your home environment, work environment, or school environment. Describe situations when you have experienced emotional or verbal abuse or something similar.

5. If you have experienced someone consistently using "you" statements, how did this make you feel? Have you

ever defined someone by using the phrases mentioned in the "No More" section?

6. Explore the definition of emotional abuse in the "Reflections" section. What aspects of that list (if any) have you experienced consistently in a significant relationship?

7. Discuss boundaries you have used that helped with your environment, even if it wasn't a consistent problem.

8. In what ways have you participated in defaming another person or used disparaging language toward another image-bearer? On social media?

9. Read Isaiah 45:4b and consider a name of honor God might have for you.

God Sighting Update:

Recently, I saw Forgiven Man out front in the parking lot. I braced myself and said a quick prayer for peace. The door opened. He stood in front of me, completely calm. I grabbed a lunch ticket to offer and, fearing what it might bring, tentatively asked, "Last name?"

Then, this beautiful man uttered his given name. He smiled. "Is there a case worker here today?"

Taken aback at first, I smiled and stood to honor him. After I explained the sign-up list for case management, he legibly wrote his given name.

"You could have some breakfast or a cup of coffee while you wait," I offered, still stunned at the miracle before me.

"No problem. I'll wait."

Later, a Lamb Center case manager assisted and cared for Binh's immediate needs. Most importantly, he was seen, known, and loved. Forgiven Man *always* had a name at The Lamb Center.

Lord of answered prayers, God of gods, You reach the nameless, the faceless, the unseen. You, Prince of Peace, calm the unrest inside each of us.

CHAPTER SIX

Victoria's Car Problems
or _Parts of Us_

*I*t is estimated that nearly 26% of all homeless Americans are mentally ill.[1] From schizophrenia to depression, bipolar disorder to suicidality. Which caused what? If you are living on the streets after some catastrophic life event, wouldn't *you* be depressed and maybe even suicidal?

Some mentally ill people on the street have family, friends, diagnoses, and medication but opt not to use (or depend on) them. They may rage on those who corner them with the hard truth of their illness. They choose to go it alone. Kill the messenger; slay the serum. They fall into homelessness because of the strength of their will and rage. They find comfort in the idiosyncrasies of their mind and turn inward. Coming in and out of the reality of everyday life, their occasional obsessional outbursts rattle out of their brains and mouths and into the public eye.

Both Sides of the Story

During my late high school years, one of my dear friends lost both her parents to cancer within a relatively short period. Though it was intensely sad for all her siblings, her oldest brother took the brunt of it. The brilliant, near-genius linguist with multiple degrees lost his cool. A pattern of odd rants and even arrests developed, and this man we knew and loved was diagnosed with schizophrenia.

In the years that followed, he was in and out of mental institutions, checking himself out and eventually becoming homeless. He forfeited family help and gave all of his money away on the streets of Miami. His siblings surmised that perhaps his years spent at a boarding school, where he was away from family and abused, coupled with the intense trigger of the loss of his parents were too much for his precious mind. He eventually lost his life to a likely suicide, homeless. I witnessed firsthand this journey from normalcy to psychosis—the plight of a caring family trying to rescue an unwilling loved one. It was heartbreaking.

And now, working alongside some of the mentally ill at The Lamb Center, I can see the plight from a guest's perspective. I see what the fallout looks like from the other side, especially in the case of a woman named Victoria.

Victoria

It is likely Victoria's situation is similar to my friend's brother's. With Victoria, you *might* have a good experience, or you might have a horrifying shouting match. You just never know what you're going to get when you encounter her.

Victoria is an attractive woman in her mid-forties, with beautiful white teeth and a winning smile. Her gorgeous big blue eyes are either wild or winsome depending on her mood. Friendly networker or stay-out-of-my-way executive. Her tan skin looks more like she has been on vacation than out on the streets. She is rather tall and fit with an athletic build, and if dressed properly, you could imagine her walking off the tennis court at a local country club.

I first met Victoria when I was volunteering at the front desk of The Lamb Center. She complimented me on my workout top, and we struck up a kind conversation about my regimen and how I stayed so fit. It was similar to a conversation with a neighbor, in that had we not been in a homeless day center, I might have asked her if she'd like to go for a run later or maybe play tennis after work. I was shaken back to reality when I complimented her on her beautiful smile. She popped out her dentures and smiled. "They're fake!"

She went on her way to get a shower and process her laundry. Afterward, she was having some intense conversations with some of the other guests who had cars. Apparently, Victoria was having some car trouble. I should have gathered from her blackened fingernails that she had attempted to fix it herself. The guys offered her suggestions and exchanged ideas. Truly, to the observer that morning, Victoria seemed like a good woman, just down on her luck.

Patti, the assistant director of The Lamb Center, filled in the missing pieces later, when I observed Victoria rudely mutter "b****" as Patti walked by. I was stunned at what seemed so out of character for the woman I'd just met, who had been so kind and engaged with me. Come to find out, a few weeks prior, The Lamb Center had gone to court to see if Victoria could be committed to a mental institution to get the help she needed. She had cut the wires in her apartment building electric box, paranoid something was coming through them. Additionally, she'd tried to flood The Lamb Center by turning on completely all the showers with the nozzles pointed outside the stalls and then left the building. She clearly posed a danger to herself and others.

Social workers and county officials familiar with the case were equally baffled when Victoria appeared in court completely cogent, intelligent, and pulled together with complete explanations for each accusation. The entire Lamb Center staff looked like *they* were crazy accusing this poor woman of ill deeds. The judge released Victoria, readily impressed with her brilliant defense and demeanor. Although she lost the apartment, her mind became "normal" at just the right moment to hide her mental illness. Victoria was left with only "justified" rage at The Lamb Center staff for reporting her.

I learned quickly firsthand that, indeed, you never know what you are going to get with Victoria in the house. On another occasion, I warmly greeted Victoria by name. She jerked her head sharply and admonished me severely under her breath, "Don't *ever* say my name out loud."

I winced. "Got it."

From then on, I checked Victoria in silently and waited for her to initiate any conversation, but even that proved unpredictable. One day, I was calmly chatting with her over some breakfast when she asked what the other guests, with the day's newspapers in hand, were talking about. To my answer, her eyes grew wide in complete panic.

Compassion swept over me as the little girl in her asked me, "Is it really true?"

I had to tell her it was true. A man in San Bernardino had gunned down his own colleagues on a corporate campus. "Yes," I said gently, adding that we were safe at The Lamb Center.

"NO ONE IS SAFE!" she screamed, her eyes darting wildly.

Patti and Dave came out of their office, ready to send her out of the building for breaking the rules with her yelling.

My eyes filled with tears at how frightened she appeared. I longed to comfort her panic. I wanted to protect her from the terrorists on the street and comfort the part of her mind that was so vulnerable and terrified. I was torn over the rules but quickly saw how other guests were being triggered by her shouting and getting agitated as well. All I could do was panic pray for her. "Jesus, please!" Thankfully, she quickly lowered her voice to mutterings and marched out the back door for a cigarette.

She *was* right. It isn't safe anywhere. Terrorists are accomplishing their mission to knock all of us off balance, unleashing fear in the most unlikely places. Honestly, don't we all want to scream at the top of our lungs over this nonsense? There is some truth and a righteous energy to the "crazy" talk, right?

Developing connections with those who are mentally ill and affirming some of their opinions with an open ear and heart can sometimes take whacky turns. Maybe you too have had a conversation that took a left turn down a rabbit trail of nonsense. It is so hard to discern mental illness at first. You start to engage and connect in conversation, then are stunned, seemingly holding an irrational piece of the person's psyche. You gradually come to realize the individual is unstable. It can happen within a single conversation. From normal to not in a matter of moments.

My heart broke again on another day, months later, when I signed for a delivery from a gourmet bakery. It was a gorgeous birthday cake for Victoria from her family. *Happy Birthday, Vicky! We love you!* it read. She stomped out when she saw it, likely still angry at her family for "betraying" her. Treachery! They were, of course, attempting to reach out again in love. Victoria, I learned that day, had a family with ample money and resources and that she had been a capable business woman with a sizable staff under her. But mental illness changed all that.

Parts

Parts of Victoria—capable, handy, funny, volatile, warm, social, reactive. It's all true. A unique prism of personality, complex and diverse. Aren't we too essentially predictable until triggered by fear or harm? Then we can become nearly unrecognizable, doing courageous or egregious things, surprising even ourselves. Or we turn in to master cover-up artists, deflecting the inside panic with dismissive explanations or becoming preoccupied with present-day issues instead of the reasons beneath the anxieties.

There are parts of Victoria—a past, a present, and a future. Clearly the past is affecting her present, which is critical to helping her into the future. Victoria's mental illness is tangled in definitions. Most professionals and researchers tell us mental illness stems from a combination of things. Brain chemistry. Trauma. Environment. Heredity. Our brains are fascinating and brilliant machines. Uniquely human. The homeless have little ability to cover up their problems, so we see Victoria raw. She is living in the present, haunted by her past, derailing her future because instead of working through her past and getting help, she would rather focus on present-day car troubles. It's so easy to see in others, isn't it?

Back to the Future

With me, it took a more conscious effort to unpack the past. I sensed a deadening of my spirit and longed to go further with God, to places I sensed Him tugging me toward in my heart. A book I'd read on storytelling compelled me to dig a little deeper.[2]

I bravely booked a flight by myself to attend The Story Workshop at the Seattle School, a seminary started in part by Dr. Dan Allender (the author of the book I had read). My passion to dig deep into my personal story sparked my wanderlust and passion for adventure too. That had been buried in Caribbean beach lounging with my husband to rest from business and the more typical once-a-year extended-family vacations. So, I meticulously planned a subsequent drive to Yellowstone National Park and the Grand Tetons. My soul needed depth and solitude. Adventure and exploration. The Holy Spirit who roamed The Lamb Center so freely had disrupted my rhythm and awakened something deep within me. I was restless in my spirit.

Since my bathroom revelation (Chapter Five) and an inspection of the emotional deficits in my life, I'd established some healthier boundaries. They brought some needed changes to my marriage. While I was adjusting to some of these changes and enjoying the new freedom, the progress focused on my husband and his story. I still needed to deal with my own story of how I ended up where I was.

Through social media, I learned my long ago Young Life leader and friend, a professional therapist with a story of her own, had just moved solo to the West Coast for an adventure from her years in the Midwest. We connected, and she offered a place to stay to prepare for the conference. I hadn't remembered that she studied under Dan Allender and was a big fan of his programs. My prelodging was all set with a safe and trusted friend, and I was happy knowing she, a professional, had vetted the conference.

Excavation and Preparation

I had a homework assignment to write a story a few months prior to the conference. We were to write an account of harm in our past, as early in childhood as we could remember. I had a difficult time thinking of one, so I decided to talk to Mom and comb through old family photo albums. Between Sunday church, weekly lunch visits, and daily phone calls, there wasn't much Mom and I didn't discuss. It seemed like no stone was left unturned.

My photo albums didn't reveal much of relevance. They contained a few odd pictures of frowning faces and scantily clad and awkward toddler shots, back from the days before the digital era to which we have become accustomed. My mom assured me I was happy at Disneyland, even though my pigtails looked too tight and my smile was turned upside down in all of the photos. I wondered, though I didn't voice it, why Mom insisted so strongly I was happy when it was obvious I wasn't. And why did Dad include so many pictures with the sour look on my face?

Dad is a meticulous historian, a librarian by trade, so he had labeled each picture—far too many. I'd always believed I was from a "good Christian home" where nothing too bad ever happened. Come to think of it, didn't my husband say his home was "picture perfect" too? Don't most of us who were "raised right," with a spanking or two, A and B grades, parents still together, and perfect church attendance make the same claim? I had nothing to report for this assignment or so I thought.

Unable to find any stories from childhood, I determined the earliest story of pain was the one I had already worked through in counseling. My mom had even sweetly apologized for her part in my pain. It was the one of me at twenty-one years old, broken-hearted (Chapter Four). That seemed to be the earliest "hardship" and that unraveled plenty to keep me busy. No sense digging further back. I decided to use that story, even though it wasn't technically from my youth. I plowed ahead with my writing, finishing it to the exact word count and on the exact deadline for submission two months before the conference. Always the hypervigilant student, I knew I was prepared for whatever I AM had planned next.

The Known and the Unexpected

My story was to be read by a facilitator, who was a trained therapist for my small group of six strangers. I had to sign off that I did not know any of the six. Although extreme, I knew this was a safety for those with all the "big" problems. I knew I was moving forward, following God with a gut instinct I had only recently really started following. I knew it would be a good experience, great training in storytelling and the art of listening at a seminary known for powerful counseling and insight.

What I didn't know was that my mom, my beloved friend, would die suddenly only two weeks before my departure.

Fresh with grief, God got my attention, deep in my soul. The sovereign God who had tugged on my heart to "go there" to places of pain in my past had known the date He would be taking my mom home, from the beginning of time. Knowing that to be true, I kept with the scheduled Story Workshop.

I revisited my story of harm with fresh insight and raw emotions, in the safety of God's perfect sovereignty. My mom was safely seeing in full what she had only known in part (1 Corinthians 13:12). She was not only seeing Jesus Himself but also her life and mine reflected perfectly and explained like quilt work.

Because she was in and with complete Peace, I could look at my own life, knowing her influence and opinion was not a concern for me any longer. It was safe and wise for me to inspect my life and see not a childhood of abuse but a grooming of saying all was well when it wasn't. Covering up others' sins against me by forgiving and performing like the perfect Christian *should*! Being a "godly" codependent, which is "a dysfunctional pattern of living that emerges from our family of origin as well as our culture, producing arrested identity development and resulting in an overreaction to things outside of us and an under-reaction to things inside of us."[3]

Although it may seem scary and painful, it *is* wise to go back to your past in your present with God to ensure your future destiny. Being bold and brave enough to dig in to the heart of the matter, to investigate your past, isn't a waste of time. The process crystallizes your vision and clarity for present difficulties and provides insight and wholeness for your future. *This* is life to the full (John 10:10b). It sets you free to *imagine* with God all He has in store for you to be and do!

Victoria had one thing right. It's best to check under the hood before your engine overheats and breaks down.

Complex Creations

As believers in God, we know He created us. Favorably so, I might add(Psalm 139:14; Hebrews 2:6–8), in the likeness of His image (Genesis 1:27). It would take thousands of chapters to fully unpack this gift of being created in the likeness of God. But what does it mean? Clearly, we are thinking, creating, emoting, relating, reasoning, rejecting, accepting, free-willing, freewheeling humans! *Imagine* that. Made in God's image. He is triune—Holy Father, Holy Jesus, Holy Spirit, three in one. We are body, soul, and spirit.

Cue Creepy Music

There is a villain to the story. To our story. To His story in us. It isn't a fairytale, one to put away on Sunday afternoon as we leave church. John 10:10 explains the full picture. The truth is, "the thief comes only to steal and kill and destroy." Dan Allender breaks that down in vivid language with regard to our places of deep wounding. Steal—to steal innocence. Kill—to kill hopes and dreams. Destroy—to shame you or show contempt for your personhood.[4]

Essentially, the thief attempts to derail your destiny. And he starts when you are very young. When you are vulnerable and trusting. Full of life and promise. Hopeful and playful. He tries to kill all this. He heaps on whispered lies about your value and worth to your soul, causing shame and cover-up. Interesting that the enemy knows exactly how to target you to prevent you from being of any use now or in the future: by keeping the treasure of his theft under lock and key. He usually attacks at the greatest level of passion or personhood. The enemy would love to have us stay locked down in our fear and anxiety. To keep the hope of healing away forever and never address it for restoration and redemption's story.

Sadly, too many Christians unwittingly play along with his tactics. They stay stuck in a culture of burying the past and are content playing in puddles instead of jumping into the ocean of opportunities God has in store for us.

Dissociation

Because we *all* encounter harm, especially during childhood, the great I AM designed our brains with a mechanism to survive. When abuse, trauma, or an event or circumstance that a child does not fully understand occurs, both limited perspective and the lack of developmental ability to process the event can cause confusion and damage. So this "escape hatch" called dissociation is indeed a lifesaver.

In order to understand your whole story, it's important that you have at least an overview of how this works. Everyone has dissociated parts of their memory. Essentially they are parts of our human experience that have not been properly processed or assimilated into our minds and stories. When memories go through regular channels in our minds, we are able to pull them up and examine them. When they are traumatic or not understood in their contexts, though, they take a different path and are inaccessible. Although it is intricately complex in scientific and physiological terms, the founder of Rescued for Destiny,

Karen Duckett, effectively describes it in layman's terms in *Rescued for Destiny Basics*:

> Dissociation is when thoughts, emotions, sensations or memories are separated from the rest of the psyche. The person (usually at a very young age) literally goes away in his or her head to flee from anxiety producing experiences from which there is no physical escape. That part of the person gets "stuck" at the age the event occurs. Depending on the severity of the event, it's as if it "never happened." However, it did happen and the person suffers and has trouble moving forward in his or her Destiny until those parts of the thinking and emotions are freed. . . There is much suffering as through the years this person tries to go forward with parts of him or her missing (like a missing comrade or partner). . . . The suffering manifests itself in different ways, including but not limited to: mental and emotional stress and shut down, feeling "stuck" in certain areas, physical ailments and disease. This robs people of their Destiny and sometimes their very life, and it is not fair! . . . The *good news* is the same God who designed our minds to separate out so we could survive is the One who is well-able to gather and put all the parts of us back together—not just to get back to zero on the number line—but for super wellness![5]

> "For this is what the Sovereign Lord says: I myself will search for my sheep and look after them. As a shepherd looks after his scattered flock when he is with them, so will I look after my sheep. I will rescue them from all the places where they were scattered on a day of clouds and

darkness.... I will search for the lost and bring back the strays. I will bind up the injured and strengthen the weak." (Ezekiel 34:11–12, 16a)

Now, there is a range of dissociation. Some of it is simple, like when you are driving down the highway lost in thought and later have absolutely no memory of getting to your destination. Then there is the extreme psychosis, called Dissociative Identity Disorder (DID), which used to be called Multiple Personality Disorder.

We are not talking about either of those extremes but about this God-designed "escape hatch" in our minds when we cannot assimilate all the negative experiences in our reality. No one is exempt! You would have had to have perfect parents, perfect siblings, perfect teachers, perfect friends, a perfect church, perfect authority figures, perfect everything in order to not have dissociated parts.

Although the story I shared at the Story Workshop was about my twenty-one-year-old self, a dissociated part of me, a six-year-old in Disneyland, showed up to share it. In my group, a member noticed my feet rubbing together. Interesting. I still catch myself doing that when I need to calm myself. Others in the group noticed my baby-like voice that came out when I was questioned about why I would call my mother for affirmation when I knew her reaction would be callous. As they revealed these aspects of my dissociated parts to me, I began to allow them into my current reality. As the six-year-old me was acknowledged by both the group and me, I could assimilate her story into mine. Although she seemingly had nothing to do with the story being told, she revealed the very reason *why* the story was being told.

This sweet child was told everything was perfect in Disneyland. "You *are* having a good time," her parents said to her, even though she was not. She was told, "You can be happy if you will yourself to be."

It is likely that my mother, with dissociated childhood parts of her own, had spent good money on the trip and dressed me to the nines and thus expected a good day at Disneyland. She shamed me into loving what I wasn't loving at all, into rejecting my true desires and accepting that this was "wonderful" when it wasn't to me. Although there was no "abuse" happening there, what occurred did cause my heart's true desires to dissociate. And it was a repeated theme in my life. Likely there are more versions of me behind the six-year-old who were likewise shamed into loving something that wasn't good at all. Maybe even something downright evil.

Though my dissociated parts (some call an "inner child") came up at a conference where I was being purposeful in a search for healing, it is much more common to have them pop up in daily life. We just need to pay attention, so we can invite God into the story for restoration. Our parts speak up through fears, obsessions, anxiety, outbursts, meltdowns, and even "stuckness." Often other loved ones trigger parts for us, especially during conflict or family gatherings.

There are years and layers to the themes of pain in our stories. The enemy (using flawed people) inflicts harm to our most tender places of promise and passion. In God's rescue mission, not only do some dissociated memories pop up, but so do the obvious agreements we made with the enemy to shut down the life and loveliness shamed so long ago. I began to let God into those deep wounds for healing and have been ever since. Such wellness has resulted from this endeavor to let I AM into those places long forgotten, deep in the heart. Only He can restore what was once lost.

Whether we like it, or not, these memories remain in the body and figuratively, deeply embedded in the heart. As Blaise Paschal, French philosopher and mathematician, so wisely said, "The heart has its reason which reason knows not of." Your frontal cortex doesn't have a clue. But the body and your soul still feel it. It seems the mind "forgets," but the memory and its effects remain, often manifesting in fear, pain, or even physical illness.

Top scientists, including Harvard's Dr. Bessel van der Kolk, a trauma specialist, believe "the body cannot lie."[6] Physical symptoms of chronic pain, headaches, heart palpitations, and breathing problems surrounding anxiety may crop up to warn our bodies of the dangers previously endured but buried in our minds. None of this is fair to our bodies and our lives. It certainly isn't healthy to keep wounded parts of us separate and buried forever in our souls.

Christian Culture Cover-up

Yet how often in Christian culture do we hear "Let bygones be bygones," "Forgive and forget," "Leave well enough alone"? How about "Don't go there" when bringing up an old family secret or wound? When we attempt to find the underlying cause of nagging anxiety or severe depression, we often feel disconnected from the church body, as if "Sunday school for losers" doesn't have a meeting room, not even in the basement alcove. We might as well stay home. Private therapy offices are where we receive the most welcome, and we pay dearly for those sessions, even within the Christian community. It seems ridiculous that countless parishioners suffer silently or in near solitude but bring their widest smiles into the community of the "fellowship" hall. Like Victoria, I pop out the dentures that make the smile and call it for what it is: FAKE!

Both our church families and our biological families may have resistance to stripping the image that "everything is fine" and "nothing happened" and going *into* these places with God. Exposure reveals truth that not many folks want to revisit. I remind you, Jesus *is* a polite disruptor! Not that we are to wreak havoc, but shutting down inspection for healing and needed change in the name of "keeping the peace" is not right. Jesus, while on earth, followed wherever His Father God led Him. He spoke out to earthly families, including his own, who were holding people back from their destinies and God-given paths (Matthew 8:18–22; 12:46–50).

God's Real-life Answers

God's first explanation of Himself was to Moses. He said in Exodus 3:14, "I AM WHO I AM. Say this to the people of Israel: I AM has sent me to you" (NLT). Essentially, He is saying, "I AM always. I was. I am. I always will be." He is the inexhaustible source of energy, the ever present source of truth and life. Jesus says in the New Testament, among many I AMs, "I AM the way, the truth and the life" and the only way to get to the Father (John 14:6). "I AM the resurrection and the life" (John 11:25). Let's insert here that the Pharisees (the local religious officials who were waiting for this Messiah Savior) gasped and declared Him a blasphemer for saying what only God could say: "I AM!"

We are a good design in a fallen world of sin—our own sin, sins against us individually, and the sin apparent in a fallen world. Eden lost. But God! Those are some of my favorite transitions in the Bible—but *God*! In all these dark places, the Light of the World remains. He is a God of redemption, and God's mission has always been "to bring good news to the poor" (and poor in spirit), "to comfort the brokenhearted and to proclaim that captives will be released and prisoners will be freed" (Isaiah 61:1 NLT). God, the great I AM, who designed our minds to separate out so we'd survive trauma and difficult circumstances is the same God who gathers and puts all these precious parts of our thinking and emotions back together. Perfectly. So we may be the whole us, not one part missing, to completely fulfill our destinies.

Let's not join the Pharisees, who promoted cover-up and shutdown. Let's dust off our real-life Bibles that contain real-life people and their stories.

> "He reached down from heaven and rescued
> me; he drew me out of deep waters. He rescued

me from my powerful enemies from those who
hated me and were too strong for me. They
attacked me a moment when I was in distress,
but the Lord supported me. He led me to a place
of safety. He rescued me because he delights in
me." (2 Samuel 22:17–20 NLT)

These difficult and horrific scenarios call for a rescuer. They
are real, and God is *the* rescuer. And not just in the here and now,
when it is happening. I AM is still present, in the past, with the
memories of harm we currently might not be able to access. God,
I AM, can access what we can't! Why would God say "I AM in
the past" if the past didn't matter? Why is history important?

It is *His* story and yours. It is relevant to your future. To something long dead in us, He says, "I AM the RESURRECTION
AND THE LIFE" (John 11:25a; emphasis mine)! Come forth!

Your Way, Truth, and Life

Is a reality from your past affecting your future? Have you
been trip wired by anger or a behavior out of control? Are you
shut down and stuck, living in a current state of blah? Are
hopes, dreams, innocence, wonder, and beauty missing from
your life? Have you ever uttered the phrases "It won't work,"
"Must be nice," "Maybe someday," "This is life as a working
stiff," or "The past is the past; move forward"? Many of us are
content in our low day-to-day expectations when we were created for much more life.

Jesus is the way, the truth, and the life (John 14:6). He is
waiting to restore us. Listen to the end of John 10:10: "My purpose is to give them a rich and satisfying life" (NLT). Life to
the full measure. Give me some of that! We know the Savior.
He saves us for heaven, yes, but Jesus said He came to give us
a *rich* and *satisfying* life, not just an afterlife! He doesn't intend
for us to have a humdrum life of servitude, duty, and avoidance
of sin. He came to give us the life we were destined to live, for
which He created us. Psalm 23:6 says, "Surely goodness and

mercy and unfailing love shall follow me ALL the days of my life, and I shall dwell forever [throughout all my days] in the house *and* in the presence of the Lord" (AMP; emphasis mine).

Jeremiah 29:11 says He came to give us "hope and a future." That is abundant joy and a destiny. And before you despair and say "It is too late," "I missed the boat," or any of the aforementioned phrases, remember Romans 8:28, that He will work it *all* together for *your* good and His glory.

The enemy has played lines and tactics so predictable we should know better. In Genesis 50:20, Joseph teaches us truth. Remember, he lived a nightmare but had a destiny and purpose to live out. His brothers, inspired by the enemy, intended evil for Joseph, *but God* (there it is again), "intended it for good to accomplish what is now being done."

This is a process for us as it was for Joseph. Our Savior is the victor over this measly opponent. He is I AM! Praise Eternal Father, Powerful Jesus, Ever-Present Holy Spirit—three in one! We are the children of the VICTOR, King of all kings, Lord of all lords! Can I get a hallelujah?!

Our Participation

Our Rescuer does, however, require us to participate in this recovery mission of our "inner children," or parts of us that got stuck in forgotten events of sabotage and destruction. We must permit the mighty Rescuer, our Savior, to come near, to enter in. Like a drowning person, we must cooperate with the lifeguard and relax. We must trust Him to come near, gently take ahold of us, and bring us to shore, to breathe fresh breath into our worn-out self. We need to inspect and assimilate the event with God. *That* is restoration.

It's all about tense, isn't it? Like Victoria, we spend so much time in the present fretting over the future that we gladly and easily forget the past. In fact, we subtly mock friends who study the impact of their pasts, because doing so seems to slow them down. Meanwhile, we pour ourselves another glass of wine, take a few more aspirin, or make color-coded calendars for our hypervigilant lives. We live busy, over-planned lives, overextending ourselves and our children, complaining all the while.

The truth is, "getting over the past," without inspecting it and combing *through* it, leads to a pattern of sin and difficulty — shifting addictions, serial dieting, bad relationships, anger issues. The many problems that arise in our lives tend to be but different embodiments of the same thing. That is, unless we get *in* to the heart of the matter. God (I AM) is waiting for us to inspect it in safety. He brings His peace, His release and relief to set the captive, tender part of you free! He brings His truth, justice and grace to that long shut-down part, releasing the goodness and original purpose of that part to your current self. We need these restored parts with us to complete our whole selves; it's restoration for our designed destinies.

Check Under the Hood

Victoria suffers from a vicious mental illness so chaotic her safety and others' safety are at risk. On a good day, like most of us, she is distracted in the present with issues of her immediate future, the car. (Yes, she drives. Bless you if you run into her around town on one of her bad days.) But when it's not a good day? Quick fear. Rage. Anger and shouting. Irrational antics. What in her brain is bouncing around causing such panic?

Hauntings of the past, I suspect. Dissociated memories. Aren't those all the telltale signs of the enemy's battle tactics? How unusually cruel to have all the toxic and terrifying reactions of Victoria scare off anyone who could help. Enemy fingerprints are all over this ravaged life.

Well-meaning family and good churches and therapists can't help a single unwilling soul who refuses to let I AM gain access. Therapists may find the story, but only I AM can rescue, heal, and restore what was stolen, killed, or destroyed. So, it's best to do spiritually and emotionally, what Victoria does literally. Check under your hood.

Tune Up the Heart and Mind

The modern psychology world and Western culture is abuzz about "mindfulness," and we Christians should be too. In Romans 12:2, Paul urges us to "be transformed by the renewing of your mind." Then, he says, we will be able to determine what God's will is—"his good, pleasing and perfect will." Sounds like God can reboot the memory and give us understanding about the will and destiny we were designed for by Him! Wow. 1 Corinthians 2:16 says, "But we have the *mind* of Christ" (emphasis mine). Believer, we need to look at the Bible in the context of personal healing. Read God's Word with fresh courage as you understand the mind and the mechanics of the past, present, and future.

Be present! It causes us to read Romans 12:1 with new insight:

> Therefore, I urge you, brothers and sisters, in
> view of God's mercy, to offer your bodies as a
> living sacrifice, holy and pleasing to God—this
> is your true and proper worship.

Welcome, Holy Spirit. I trust you. Show me what we have here. What do I need from this part of me stuck in fear and pain? Release her. Rescue her, Jesus.

God promises that when we ask for wisdom He will give it without reserve (James 1:5). He also promises He will never leave or forsake us (Deuteronomy 31:6; Matthew 28:20). He longs for us to invite Him into all the places in our heart, all our hidden motives and thoughts (Psalm 139:23).

We can trust I AM in His perfect timing to bring up the past in our present for our future benefit. It starts with a willingness to let Him into these dark places we have put away for so long. What are you waiting for?

[The fullness of the process of identifying and rescuing parts is detailed in a six-part video series called "God's Design and

Plan: For Survival, Rescue, and Fulfilling our Destinies" on
Rescued for Destiny - Joel 2 Army's YouTube channel.]

Questions to Ponder:

1. Do you have a friend or family member with a mental
   illness? If so, carefully and respectfully share the story
   and the possible tragedy involved. If not, share an
   encounter with a person you either knew was mentally
   ill or you realized was mentally ill after a conversation
   (like Victoria and the news discussion).
2. Do you know anyone who acts like Jekyll and then
   Hyde? At your workplace or in your social circles? How
   have you handled the disparity?
3. What stories do you tell or hear about your childhood
   (if any)? What kind of stories are they (happy, sad,
   funny)? Does your family agree with your perceptions
   of the events?
4. What is your earliest memory of a story of harm?
   How have you uncovered that hurt in order to experience healing?
5. Share an example of simple dissociation of forgetting
   how you got somewhere.
6. Have you ever had a dissociated part come up out
   of nowhere? If so, can you think through a possible
   trigger? Did you try to forget it, or did you inspect it?
   Did you talk to God or someone else about it?
7. What does it mean to you to be an image bearer of God?
   Have you thought about that in regard to other people
   or people groups? How does that affect your daily life,
   your political life, your social life, your family life?
8. What part of the section "Christian Culture Cover-up"
   resonated with you and your life? Have you ever shut
   yourself or someone else down, dismissed a feeling/

problem, or covered up a clue of a more serious problem? Explain.

9. Have you ever felt like you didn't belong in church because of the problems in your past affecting your present? Explain.

10. Are you in a current state of blah? Do you know anyone who has said any of these hopeless phrases and lives a life of complacency (in "Your Way, Truth, and Life" section)?

11. What was your reaction to "God's Real-life Answers?" Do you think I AM cares about your past, your present, and your future? Is the Bible relevant to your everyday life?

12. Where is God leading you to dig up the past? How will you challenge the status quo and go deeper into reasons for an ongoing problem or theme in your life?

13. What do you think about the word *mindfulness*? How have you practiced it in your Christian journey of faith? What do you think about inspecting "under the hood?"

CHAPTER SEVEN

Erin's Death Experience or *The Living Dead*

*M*ost situations of people at The Lamb Center are fairly predictable. Something happened to them. They made a series of choices. And oddly, despite their many different cultures, creeds, shapes, and sizes, they look like, well, homeless or poor people. On a cruel, cold spring day, like in this particular March, you can picture them much like Emma Lazarus did:

> Give me your tired, your poor,
> Your huddled masses yearning to breathe free,
> The wretched refuse of your teeming shore.
> Send these, the homeless, tempest-tossed, to me:
> I lift my lamp beside the golden door.[1]

For a while I might have said all people at The Lamb Center looked every bit that description.

That is, until I met Erin. I was surprised when she checked in as a guest. By her appearance I had suspected she was a kitchen volunteer late for breakfast duty. (Many female volunteers don't get the memo that you really shouldn't look too darling in a homeless day shelter.) Erin's adorable baseball cap over her auburn Irish hair didn't match the huddled masses of

The Lamb Center guests, nor did the skinny jeans, stylish coat, and fresh white sneakers that adorned her tiny frame.

What stunned me next—but meshed up with the whole March St. Patrick's Day theme—was that she was drunk. At 8:00 a.m. check-in. This young woman reeked of alcohol.

"I used to be cute like you," she said, wobbly on her feet. I was befuddled, thinking she was the pretty one. I introduced myself.

To be honest, I should have reported her for being drunk. It is a rule that we have a "clean and sober environment," but she knocked my sound judgment off balance, much like a cold blast on an early spring day.

As she made her way to her storage locker, she passed the director, Dave.

Like with most issues of life, once you have struggled with one, you can spot people in a similar process a mile away. Dave, a recovering alcoholic, has been sober for over sixteen years now and is an inspiration to many in recovery. I saw him kindly take Erin to the side and talk to her softly.

"Man, I can't catch a break!" she slurred loudly to Dave as she stumbled back out the front door. Dave had asked her to leave.

You think Netflix series are exciting? Come see real life up close! Spellbound and holding the proverbial remote, like I had just stumbled across her series, I needed to know what episodes I had missed about Erin. This is riveting real-life drama and tragedy, people. We don't need the make-believe drama of television! After my shift, I entered Dave's office to inquire about her and he filled me in.

Years ago, Erin was raped at gunpoint. A thief had broken into her apartment, part of a rash of break-ins. Because of her odd schedule as a cocktail waitress, she was at home and in bed. Unfortunately, because she was vulnerable, she was viewed as an additional "opportunity." The thief stole much more than property. He took her safety and her soul, ravaging her peaceful sleep and replacing it with endless nightmares.

There was a violent struggle, which included her tiny frame grasping for life. She grabbed a beer bottle from the nightstand and hit him on the head. Although he left the scene without firing his weapon, the DNA evidence he left behind was found by police. The murderous thief and rapist was caught, arrested, charged, and incarcerated. Justice.

But so many solved crimes that seem like the end of the story are not. There are loose ends. The victim blinks, bewildered and forgotten. That was the case for Erin. She told a caseworker who was helping her move forward after this crime, "I *died* that night." And ever since, she has anesthetized her pain with alcohol and filled her body with false lovers, who continue the now consensual harm. She has become the walking dead.

My future encounters with Erin were sporadic. I saw her once, hopeful and excited. Working with a case worker, she'd landed a great job waiting tables. We discussed tipping and my experience of waiting tables back in the day when my husband and I were struggling to start our business. There *is* something really exhilarating about having a pocketful of cash you have earned because folks deemed your service good, great, or exemplary. She gloried in the old days when she could bring in a good profit. Her assessment that she didn't look as good because she couldn't afford the necessary root touch-ups on her glorious head of hair didn't stop her from hoping. She said, "I'm a good waitress. They are lucky to have me."

Whenever anyone at The Lamb Center takes a positive step forward, the efforts are celebrated. Such joy. It reminds me of the rejoicing in heaven over one repentant sinner (Luke 15:7). It looks simple on the outside, but oh the glory in moving forward! Even if they are simple beginnings, God loves them (Zechariah 4:10).

Sadly, my joy for Erin was short-lived. I learned she was fired from her new position because she'd shown up drunk. Although she had started AA and the new job simultaneously, she quickly fell off the wagon and back into unemployment.

The Fog of Cover-up

Watching Erin cover up her pain with alcohol, making a sad problem even worse, was frustrating. I was rooting for her to get to the heart of the matter, but she kept heaping salt on wounds, adding bondage to her heartbreak. Regular life became impossible to live. Triple tragedy.

It made me think about my own life. Erin's problems and cover-up were obvious to me. But what obvious forms of cover-up did others observe in me? What was my roadblock to moving forward into the destiny God planned for me? What kept me stuck? Was I covering up something God wanted to deal with first so I could move forward into the fullness of life?

Usually cover-up looks nice or numbs pain. That is why it is the prevalent and preferred "solution" to our problems. Projecting a certain image (that isn't the real you) is one way. Spinning the scenarios and current situations to look better than they are is another. Anyone on Facebook knows this to be true. It isn't called *Face*book for nothing—saving face? Or just a facade?

Cover-up causes a hollowness, a deadness to real life. The thing Erin was trying to get away from—the awful feeling of being the living dead—was the very thing her cover-up was doing to her. It was killing her. Killing all God was calling her to be.

Sober and clear-headed environments, just like The Lamb Center, are essential for all of us to assess the real problem. To bring healing to any deep wounds, which manifest as current-life deadness, we need to look below the surface to what's really going on.

Sticky Stuff

Many of us have "poisons" we pick to cover our hurt. Maybe yours is performance, or shopping, or eating, or gaming, or socializing, or sex. In and of themselves, none of them are bad, but if we continue to use them to cover up our problems, they stick to our souls and lead to a feeling of deadness in life.

In his book *The Journey of Desire*, John Eldredge states the complicated matter simply: "The fact is . . . we have only three options: 1. To be alive and thirsty, 2. To be dead, or 3. To be addicted. There are no other choices. Most of the world lives in addiction; most of the church has chosen deadness. . . . Every addiction comes from the attempt to get rid of the ache."[2]

Regarding alcoholism, Dave always says, "Everyone has to find their own personal low to get to AA (the help they need)." I can expand that truth and say, "Everyone has to find the bottom of the cover-up to find the hurt underneath." To take the sticky note off and read the memo beneath, so to speak.

Take Two Aspirin

Just like a hangover is double the pain because it includes regret, so are the complications that addictions add to root problems. Sadly, I had little future contact with Erin, unless she called in to The Lamb Center, usually with slurred speech.

She tried to keep me on the phone if Dave was unavailable. She went on and on about her troubles, never mentioning the one about alcohol. Usually about another abusive boyfriend who stole her money or her few possessions. There was always the additional pain of eviction and then homelessness. She lost the privilege to drive because of so many DUIs, so she was unable to get to The Lamb Center on a consistent basis.

Dave did take a few of her calls, and his response was always the same: "You need to get sober first, Erin." She knew, like most of us do, that when painkillers wear off, it *really* hurts. The underlying pain is exposed and laid bare.

Like Erin, instead of dealing with various hurts that others delivered to me, I covered them over, reconnecting with each person *without* addressing and resolving the pain they caused. I just pretended it didn't hurt, and kept up appearances. Although alcohol wasn't my cover-up, and my "death" wasn't violent like Erin's, God used the month of March to bring up the old wounds. Apparently, He wanted me to feel the death, the reality, of these three relationships. He wanted to reside in those spaces of my heart I had not opened to Him for healing. Like with Jesus, sometimes the most impactful life and renewal can't happen unless death comes first. Just like the first Easter. Crucifixion came first.

Like snow in spring, it felt every bit as cruel. It felt like death to daffodils.

Volatile March

Spring is my favorite season. In our area, the blossoms are the sweetest thing ever, heralded and celebrated with a cherry blossom festival to beat the band.

I was once embarrassingly quoted as saying (before I knew anything of sex), "I love spring; it makes me so horny!" I know. Incredibly naïve and innocent, but don't you *feel* joy of want and desire during spring? The season the Creator designed and artistically painted? The colors and hope and love and a future? Amazing season. Eternal Eden. Spring. Sweet sigh.

The start of it, however, is a bit of an anomaly.

"In like a lion; out like a lamb," the folklore says. To illustrate those extremes, God gave me my firstborn son in March many years ago. Due on the Ides, born on the twelfth, he is a beautifully hopeful human being with sparkling eyes and a winsome spirit and has been from the beginning.

We brought Dylan home from the hospital on a seventy-five-degree sunny day, nearly killing him in protective layers because of the heat, which defied the odds. A year later, his first birthday ushered in the blizzard of '96, with thirty-six inches of snow.

So hope and beauty can often be upset by a cold blast of wintry weather. Heavy sigh.

As I write this, various trees, shrubs, and ornamental grasses are getting a huge, purposeful death blow. Even hopeful limbs starting to blossom are getting a big whack back, both from the snow this March and purposeful pruning. I feel their pain. It's mine this season.

But this time around, unlike Erin, I refuse to cover up the pain. I refuse to try to restore the treasures with my own efforts. I choose to live out the death, under God's direction and protection.

To be clear, I told God, "I'm all in. I want to go all the way with Your ways." And He takes us at our word. I want to participate in all the things God is working on for His plans and purposes in my life, including my wholeness, even if the identifying and stripping of the cover-up hurts. Even if getting to the heart of the matter feels like death. I want to flourish and be the fullest me God designed from the beginning of time.

Jesus' Counterintuitive Instruction

When Jesus foretells his own death in Matthew 16:22, Peter reprimands him, saying "May God forbid it! This will never happen to you" (AMP). In verse 23, Jesus says to Peter's proclamation, "Get behind me, Satan! You are a stumbling block to Me; for you are not setting your mind on things of God, but on things of man."

Whoa! What did He say? First, He is saying not that Peter is Satan but that his words were satanic, a temptation, and pure evil. Jesus was not to avoid death but to lean into it, to do it all. Of course, we know the sweet end of this story, which goes on for eternity. Death *needed* to happen to Jesus for the epic salvation plan of God. Jesus, thank You. All glory and honor and praise be to You, Lord Christ!

That is so Sunday morning righteous (just like the birth of my precious son)! Before you get right to glorious Easter morning and get out your best spring dress or suit and get ready for the Easter egg hunt, there is more. Jesus said, "If any of you wants to be my follower, you must turn from your selfish ways, take up your cross, and follow me. If you try to hang on to your life, you will lose it. But if you give up your life for my sake, you will save it. And what do you benefit if you gain the whole world but lose your own soul? Is anything worth more than your soul?" (Matthew 16:24–26, NLT). That is a mouthful, deep and rich. We usually put this in a category for those poor disciples who had to walk those dusty roads and lived in the complicated times after Jesus' ascension. But it is for *us*. Death must come to us first if we are to fully live.

Deadly Heart Wounds

It is excruciatingly painful, my "cross." I suppose Jesus didn't call them "crosses" to be poetic, but rather graphic. He understands more than we can possibly imagine that death is unnaturally ugly business. Death is also inexplicably lonely. Between us and God.

It was a brutal death for me. I didn't expect it to hurt so much. God did a strategic extraction. He wanted to reside in a place of my heart where three people who, in various ways had hurt my sacred heart, were lodged. They were all soul-type connections. One had wounded my heart. One had rejected my heart. And one had resisted my heart. In response, I had covered each up, spun it as "fine" and "forgiven" and moved on without addressing the pain. Jesus understood each of those pains. He and I needed to take my heart back. Together we needed to cry for this sacred heart—mine.

My heart is especially important to God, as is your heart, dear one. But my heart is important to me too—the inner sanctum of me, a very holy place. I had to let God into my holy of holies, so to speak, where He wanted to reside and deserved all access.

Because this part of my story is deeply personal, I'll share only that these three important and uniquely special relationships had to "die." And I honestly felt like *I* died with them. God addressed them all at once. The relationships will never be the same. They have all perished for now. Necessary endings.

I can truly say I understand, at least in part, what Erin meant by "I died that night." Different than weeds which must die (like sin), these relationships were sweet blossoms of my life. They had each run their course. But I did not miss the timing of lent, the solemn, contemplative season before Easter, when we give up the things we love most.

Who knows if our sovereign God answered specific prayers for each of them by the removal of me? God knows. Could He resurrect any of them? Yes, if the others are willing to participate. Will He? Will they? I don't know. But God knows!

My responsibility was listening to what He was saying to me: "Take up your cross, DeeAnn, and follow *Me!*"

I will not forfeit my soul. I will love the Lord my God with *all* my heart, and all my soul, and all my mind (Matthew 22:37).

Comparing Pain

Many of us have a habit of diminishing our own pain and loss. If I were to compare my "death" to Erin's, for example, I might minimize the place in my heart where God wanted to go with me. It's always important not to compare your pain to another's pain. "All pain and human suffering is compared to Eden, not to each other," Dan Allender once wisely suggested.[3]

Each person's cross is as unique as they are. Like mine, usually it is a deep, sacred secret between God's spirit and our own spirit. He knows. We don't usually know what it is until we pick it up, carry it, and follow Him. When we do, we share deep connection and communion with Jesus, the fellowship of His sufferings (Philippians 3:10). We get just a hint of the name He will give us when we meet Him face-to-face (Revelation 2:17). Our God-given identity. Our true self.

Proper Mourning

My dear friend Judy told me long ago, when we were discussing the pace of life and my frenetic movement without stopping to feel, "If you haven't stayed in your pajamas for a few days, you haven't experienced God's freedom to be real!"

I used to be completely type A and the doer of all things (like most people in our area and many around the country). Imagine wearing pajamas for three straight days. I didn't even do that when my mom died. Then again, with actual funerals there is too much to do and so many people to share the mourning with. Like the gathering at Mary and Martha's house for Lazarus' death. Three days—that's sort of biblical, right? So I did it.

Shack Attack

God is still kind amid grief and sorrow. He knows I am weak and tend to flock to quick fixes and positive spins. First, He gave me space and time to mourn. To be real with precious saints He ordained to walk me and talk me through this pain.

He renewed an old friendship, delivered a completely new friendship seemingly out of nowhere, and coincidentally canceled another dear friend's trip (because of the late snowstorm), so I had a soul friend to be with for sweet times of prayer, tears, laughs, wine, and whine together.

The movie *The Shack* came to theaters that week as well. It is a beautiful story of a man named Mack going to his place of pain, the shack where his daughter was murdered. It was his cross of sorrow. Going to meet God in those places of pain is how his restoration begins. The cinematic beauty of this film was sweet to my soul. It gave me a glimpse of what is on the other side of death. Of crosses. Of what comes on Sunday mornings. And of what is meant to come in springtime.

And in case you were wondering, no, I did not go to the showing in my pajamas!

Come Forth

Augustine once said that if Jesus hadn't called Lazarus by name, all the dead would have responded to His command! In His Word, I maintain He is calling us *all* to "come forth." Come forth and let life come out of those places of death. "Come forth" is a life-giving, life-replenishing call.

In Erin's case, her tragic life event, which was unjust and unfair, left her lifeless. To date, she still hasn't gone there with God. She won't open up those places of pain and death to let God's life-giving Spirit in (John 4:14). It isn't easy. Sadly, she has only further buried herself in alcohol addiction (her cover-up) and desecrated her own burial tomb. As C.S. Lewis aptly asked, "Why are all sacred places dark places?"

We can't be raised for newness of life to the full until we relinquish all in our heart to Him who can resurrect *anyone* and anything from the grave!

March came in like a lion, bringing the harsh reality of death and a cross.

But GOD! *But God!* He brings March out like a lamb. Jesus, Lamb of God, God of The Lamb Center, the Restorer of all things. He restores our sacred hearts on earth for our ultimate destiny to reign with Him for eternity.

The Choice is Yours

Precious friends, what is the lion of your soul? What are you using to cover it up? What is the cross you need to pick up and carry to follow God into your destiny?

Trust the risen Savior of Easter morning to go to your wounded, aching heart. To whatever you have locked in there. Don't stay stuck in death like Erin. Move forward to follow Jesus. Embrace the death of things He shows you need to die. Release it all to Him who is faithful and true (Revelation 19:11). We can trust Him because He is able to do abundantly more than we can ever pray, or hope, or dream (Ephesians 3:20). As you do, *imagine* where He will lead you—into the desires, destiny, and calling He planned for you from the beginning of time!

Questions to Ponder:

1. What's your favorite season and why? Which season speaks to you most about God's attributes?
2. How would you describe the homeless in your town? Were you ever surprised to learn someone was homeless?
3. What's your relationship with alcoholism? Does it run in your family? Do you or do you know someone who deadens pain with alcohol?
4. What kind of pruning has God done with you? Has there been a season of cutting something off or back that has permitted a moving forward afterward?
5. Have you ever walked back into a painful season to relive the pain and mourn the loss of something to your heart? Discuss the feelings and experience.
6. How has God been kind to you amid sorrow or mourning?
7. What are some of your crosses? Take some personal time to reflect on this concept.
8. Is there something or someone that has taken over your heart in a negative or damaging way that God is nudging you to inspect? Explain.
9. What kind of cover-up wasn't mentioned in this chapter that you have either used or see used? Which of the ones mentioned have you used and to cover what?

CHAPTER EIGHT

Brian's Predicament
or <u>*Dream Weaver*</u>

*B*rian was an infrequent guest at The Lamb Center. In fact, the first time I met him I was confused because, a little like Erin, he looked like a volunteer. He was a young Asian man, well-groomed and handsome. His impressive North Face coat made him stand out from the rest of the more shabbily dressed regulars. If any of the others had picked a designer coat out of a clothing donation bin, it was already tattered and dirty from overuse.

"May I help you?" I asked, sure he was signing in from a local college ministry to serve lunch.

"I just need to check for mail."

Surprised, I quickly shifted gears and checked the mail folders. A few letters, some addressed to "Bae." Brian quickly explained that was his given name but that he went by Brian. There was also a package waiting for him in Director Dave's office. I hustled back to the front desk from Dave's office, anxious to see if Brian would open and reveal what was in the rather large box.

Most guests are thrilled with small packages, which usually contain their "Obama phones," long-awaited medications, or identification cards for which they applied. On the contrary, they generally roll their eyes at hospital bills, or any bills for that matter, and pitch them into the trash. The most despised mail is legal correspondence from family support of Fairfax County. It seems the Department of Social Services finds it hard to collect child support from someone who is homeless. In fact, most volunteers hang up on the robocalls and collection agency calls "recording our conversations" because we usually can't locate a guest being hounded down for money. Many guests don't ask for mail, as it is usually bad news or something they can't emotionally or otherwise handle.

I was thankful Brian stayed to open his package. His voice seemed dark and cynical as he did. "Another North Face. The last thing I want," he mocked. "Can you believe it?"

"Ah, no I can't!" *Heck, I'll take it*, I thought. My son would be thrilled with a new North Face jacket. I didn't dare say so, though, as it was clear hurt was underneath the disgust in his voice.

He lingered near the front desk. I invited him to get some coffee or something from the breakfast table about to be cleared for Bible study. He declined, citing his allergies to gluten and other chemicals, which made his diet a struggle while homeless. Most donations are littered with gluten, high carbohydrates, and loads of sugars. They're cheap, and yes, filling and hearty for sure, but they're not always healthy. Not a lot of fruits, vegetables, and proteins come in, especially for breakfast, because donors are often people trying to get temptations out of their homes. When healthy donations do come in, usually from a high-end organic grocery store with expiration dates looming, the guests are grateful. They eat heartily of the healthy choices that don't leave them with that brain-drain, carb-loaded feeling.

Brian described his situation briefly. He was an actor, a huge theater fan. His family, affluent and influential in evangelical circles, wasn't so sure this interest went well with their handsome and smart son. They suggested other higher callings that were clearly more godly, like preaching, working with the family business, or something more academic. Not theater. *That* was for "gays." Concerned his dabbling in the world of theater and makeup for boys was dangerous, they warned him about a path toward sin and a life of homosexuality, an "abomination."

Ironically, his family used acting as a marketing ploy for their business, a gym and Taekwondo studio. Brian's overbearing father had taught each of his children the martial arts from a young age. To promote the studio, especially among their large church membership, they performed shows for young children at Christian camps and fairs. As the family chopped bricks with bare hands and kicked through boards with brute strength and focus of mind, audiences were wowed. The show paired Scriptures on the armor of God with the strength of their training in an attempt to register more martial arts students. Young and impressionable, Brian was among the sales team of actors along with his obedient siblings.

Something clearly struck a chord with acting. It became Brian's dream to be a famous actor. Acting, although a noble calling, is not a high-paying or easily landed dream; it is often treated more like a hobby. And because neither the hobby nor the career would be tolerated in Brian's family, he opted for living on the streets.

I was skeptical about this story at first, but I did remember that one piece of mail was from an acting guild in Baltimore. Interesting. Brian admitted he hadn't landed too many actual speaking parts yet. Mind you, he was paid to be an extra on multiple movie sets in the Baltimore area. He had been right behind a famous actor in a political series filmed locally. He got paid well for standing behind someone famous and holding a clipboard all day. As a member of the acting guild, he received a stipend for his time in the production, even if it was cut. Being inside a studio all day, with plenty to eat, a stipend, and a little camaraderie, sure beat the evenings behind the dumpster of a church.

Brian knew all about various denominations and about most of the local churches. He knew about their reputations and kindness, or lack thereof. I was heartbroken as he explained that one church, at first tolerant and kind (even bringing him food and a few blankets), eventually called the police to have him removed. Parishioners are more fond of putting money into an offering plate for such a cause as homelessness and a lot less fond of getting the reputation of being "dumpy" because they have vagrants in their parking lot.

Brian moved from church to church looking for a safe place to sleep, figuring God must protect these sacred places. He grew up knowing all things religion, chapter and verse. Every Sunday, although homeless, he would dress up and attend the service of the church where he was staying. On one occasion, in another church, during the "passing of the peace of Christ," Brian started talking to an older woman and felt seen and particularly human. She smiled, and as she gave him a hug, a man rushed over and said, "Mother, that's a homeless person. He lives behind the church." Brian was mortified and instantly shamed out of the sanctuary and on to another church location.

In Between Jobs

Months passed before I saw Brian again at The Lamb Center. The next time he showed up, it was for another mail pickup. Again, he refused food, but he did ask for some canned goods from the pantry, as they were more predictable and had specific ingredients listed. After I hustled to the pantry and brought back some choices for him to consider, I asked if he'd received any more acting roles or bit parts.

"Yeah, that's where I've been. Down in Richmond. It was a crappy part, but at least I got paid…eventually." He studied the sides of each can and placed some back in front of me.

"What do you mean, wasn't it legit?" I asked.

"No. It was ok, but my part got cut—again. At least I got to hang out in the studio, which was convenient. I just needed to get paid before I could buy my Greyhound ticket back here."

Amazed by his resolve and courage to overcome so many obstacles, I offered a meager, "I'm so sorry for the hassle, but I'm really glad to see you again, Brian."

He thanked me for the canned goods, although he only found three that worked with his restrictions.

He turned to leave, then turned back again. "You may not see me for a while. I have some jobs lined up in Annapolis." Seeing my reassurance through a broad smile, he squinted with a gleam back at me. "I have this idea. So, tell me if you think it's totally crazy." His hands began to join his words with gestures of excitement. "Ok. I learned to sail when I was a kid. I totally loved it and was pretty good. So, I found a good deal on an old boat in a marina up there. I think I can afford it after just a few more parts. It'd be a heck of a lot cheaper than an apartment. And I could just live on the water! Cool, or what?" His whole expression lightened as his idea took flight.

"No, not crazy," I nodded with a sincere, "considering it" face. "Really interesting idea, Brian." Just then the phone rang. I held up my finger for Brian to wait a minute as I answered. Instead, he gathered the canned goods and left. As I watched him walk away, I was skeptical. Sailboats?

That is, until a few weeks later. I was taking in the mail and saw return addresses for a marina in Annapolis and various maritime mailings, which indicated he had, indeed, bought himself a boat. Astonishing. He actually did it!

Sail Away to Dreams

My mind floated to a place of dreams. Although Brian desired to be an actor and loved sailing, *had* he followed God's lead in how to get there? Who puts dreams in our hearts? What happens when we drop everything and go after our hearts' callings? So often Christian culture tells us our hearts are wrong, using either Jeremiah 17:9–10 or Ephesians 4:22 for backup, suggesting our hearts are deceitful and our desires corrupt us. We often silence the yearnings of our heart and name them sin or else rebellion. It's as if when we follow Jesus we are supposed to have more noble or different dreams. Never trust your heart or emotions—is *this* what I AM, the Creator and Master of the universe and beyond, meant?

As early as 1 Kings 3, we see that God asks Solomon what his heart's desire is so *Solomon* may answer Him. God doesn't command him or us to feel a certain way but rather asks us about our feelings. Christian culture has twisted this. Our God is very interested in our interactions with Him, our participation in the journey.

Psalm 37:4 seems to show that when we follow and delight in God, He gives us our hearts' desires. Doesn't it seem like He wants us to be in sync with what He created us to do, what our hearts that are in love with and submitted to Him want to do? Christian culture has driven this out of the narrative. Must we all seemingly look alike and follow in lockstep with the protocol of suburban dreams of houses on cul-de-sacs, destination weddings, 2.5 well-behaved kids, and a volunteer ministry in Sunday school?

If Jesus, Son of Man, Son of God, left his family of origin (on earth) to pursue His calling, why is it deemed an epic failure when we do the same? After all, the children of God are led by the Spirit of God (Romans 8:14). Is it better to speculate, wait too long, and miss the proverbial boat? Can you miss the opportunity for the dream if you don't listen for God's lead? At what point in life do we start acting on our ambitions and taking personal responsibility for our decisions? And if those choices differ from what our parents want for us, how and at what age do we reconcile what God wants versus what our parents deem best for us? Jesus seemed to already have the notion at age twelve (Luke 2:49).

Back in the day, a few fishermen left their boats and their nets and followed a man they didn't seem to know. His name was Jesus. A dream, a vision, or just a good hunch? Crazy, right? Not sensible. Even if some scholars who say those fishermen may have known Jesus are right, the idea of leaving a practical living and your father's business certainly is risky. But those disciples radically changed the world by walking away from sensibility, walking into homelessness, and walking on earth with the Son of God.

Joseph had prophetic dreams and made the mistake of sharing them with the wrong people, his jealous older brothers (Genesis 37). Joseph's life ended up being a *nightmare* in order for those dreams to actually come true! Isn't that often true in our lives too? We have a vision for how things could be. Ideas. Dreams. And inevitably, they often do come to pass but look nothing like we imagined. We might not have picked the means by which our dreams finally come to fruition, but God uses every bit of the journey all the same.

Stories like the disciples' and Joseph's are biblical accounts of real human beings with dreams and callings that no one deemed normal. These accounts were recorded in the Word of God to be shared for our benefit. We are no different than those who risked everything. We are no different than those broken vessels of long ago. We too can be real and faithful.

Even Jesus Himself was thought to have a screw loose by His own family, and He opted for the "adoption" of spiritual brothers and sisters instead of cleaving to the societal norms and familial bonds. He had a higher calling for sure. He was about His Father's business (Luke 2:49). It wasn't until after Jesus' resurrection that His brothers, James and Jude, came to belief in Jesus as the Christ (Jude 1).

You Can Be Anything You Want To Be

Most parents give in to the "Be whatever you want; dream all you dare to dream" line for their children. And to some extent, the power of the dream paired with positive encouragement and, of course, natural skills and inclinations can bring about Olympic athletes, amazing authors, and passionate artists. However, it doesn't usually work out like that.

As I ponder God's design in all this, I ask myself, "What were my hopes and dreams as a child? What was I destined to do as a vocation? What did God place in my heart of hearts when He said He had a plan for me?" An intelligent design suggests He might make things go *with* the grain of my proclivity instead of completely against it. What about God's desire for

97

a royal priesthood and a holy nation (Exodus 19:6, 1 Peter 2:9, Revelation 1:6)? How do I figure into what God Himself desires and deserves? He has dreams for the people who know Him. He wants us to participate in great exploits with Him (Daniel 11:32). God's heart and my heart meet together for a one-of-a-kind passion and purpose in His kingdom.

Sometimes living in the what's expected and the what's next keeps us stuck in complacency and on the treadmill of life. Don't so many adults live glazed-over lives, hating what they do, waiting for the weekend? Brian's decision would never be called "wise" or "thoughtful"—more likely "insensible" and "ridiculous"—but why? What's preferable: safe and boring or a little over-the-edge and following the dream?

My mom was a master teacher (which was her dream, by the way). She was glowingly popular with students and parents alike, winning the Teacher of the Year award at her traditional public school in an influential county. I learned most notably through her death that she was very good at developing the dreams of her students. She opened their impressionable minds to "be all they could be" while also teaching the hard work, dedication, and optimism required to do so. Among the third-grade students she once taught are savvy Wall Street business people, Broadway actors, professional ballerinas, lawyers, doctors, and teachers. Many thank my mom for inspiring them to pursue their dreams. My brother even credits our mom for guiding him into engineering, which he had a knack for. She told him, "You can do it! Work hard. Pursue your dream!" Essentially "you do you". Go for it!

My parents were big proponents of experiences, making the most of every opportunity and making sure we received a college education. They encouraged hard work and doing our best.

Studies abroad? Go for it! I did. It so expanded my love for people and love of God's creation and richly enhanced my personal faith in Christ.

An audition for the campus show choir? Do it! I did and didn't make it. Apparently, my singing voice and sight-reading are far sweeter than my knack for learning dance steps!

Start a concierge business? Go for it! Wait, it wasn't my idea; it was my successful Christian boyfriend's idea. My parents thought it was a great opportunity, though, because they suspected it might solidify the relationship. But it was *his* dream. It *was* a great opportunity. I did it. I learned much as an entrepreneur and learned a lot about hard work and doing absolutely everything I had *never* imagined myself doing. Looking back at the lessons learned and skills acquired along the way, I can't say I would do it again, but I am proud of all we accomplished over many years of hard work.

Twisted in those hopes and dreams was a preconceived notion of what a Christian girl *should* do. Have a lovely traditional wedding, marry a successful Christian man (preferably with a heritage of Bible-believing folks), raise college-bound children, remain well-connected in the community, and be sure the entire family is involved visibly at church—ahem, your parents' church. And on it goes. I don't know if this is latent sexism or a directive, but my hopes and dreams had to coincide with what my parents envisioned for me. It was never said, but it was expected. It was the "should" of my Christian culture.

What escaped my conscious thought is that I had a choice. I think I was more driven to make everyone happy with my choices than I was driven to inspect my own sacred heart. The one God created, designed, and planned a future for.

God's Will Be Done

Although calling myself a successful business woman, homemaking wife, mother, and volunteer is amazingly satisfying, it isn't quite all I am or all I dreamed I could be. That one sentence was much easier to write than it was to accomplish! Much of that happened only to keep up appearances. It is exhausting work to meet the expectations of others—the image someone else thinks is best for you.

After stripping away much of my image buildup, I can see that the qualities and desires God placed in me indeed have been used throughout my life and now expand into more fullness with my wellness.

I *am* a mother through and through. And in that is a *teacher* through and through. Those heart desires have come to pass and continue through the "mothering" of other Christian women, friends, and my adult children. I am a communicator through and through. Over the years I have taught employees, trained managers, and shared spiritual and biblical knowledge in community groups and at church. Because of my pursuit of God and the pursuit to know more of my truest self, I am expanding those gifts into new dreams!

My passion for communication and teaching led me to write this book. I continue to teach and communicate to groups, including at The Lamb Center, through my story, all God has done to heal and grow me.

I am creative (I think *all* of us are creative, as we are created in the image of an amazingly creative God). I enjoy making lovely spaces in my home. I engage others and love people, inviting them into my space and into my home with hospitality. I enjoy inviting people in, just like Jesus does. The wanderlust, a part of my personality, has been satisfied to some extent through vacations. But the more I flow into my own dreams, using the experiences of the past, the more I am excited about the explosive growth ahead. Places to explore are expanding. God delights in and lives in our hearts, so He gladly shouts, just as Dr. Seuss does, "Oh the places *we'll* go!"[1]

"God's will be done." As Jan Karon in the *Mitford* series through Brother Tim said, it's "the prayer that never fails."[2] It took me fifty years to get that right! Heck, Moses was eighty when he spoke to Pharaoh about letting God's people out of bondage. Joseph was seventeen when he had his prophetic dreams and probably close to fifty by the time they were actualized.

I am reminded of the *always* promise of God. Romans 8:28 says, "And we know that God causes *everything* to work together for the good of those who love God and are called according to his purpose for *them*" (NLT; italics mine). I never looked at a pronoun so carefully as I have recently. It's for *me*. It's for *my* good. And for *you* and *your* good. Yes, God's purpose, but for *our* good. As I see the character of God asking people like Solomon, and Hagar, and Eve, and the woman at the well, and those He healed what they were feeling, where they were, where they were going, and what they wanted, I get excited. Isn't that the same God now? Doesn't He want to intersect with our desires to work *all* things together for *our* good and *His* glory? I think so! *Imagine!* "God's will be done" is us being and doing what He designed us to be and to do. That includes the odd ways we finally get to the heart's desire, the destiny and dream, the hope for our future.

Aspirations

Although I haven't seen Brian since his adventure to Annapolis, I pray he has discovered the beauty of God's favor as he follows his dreams. Brian had stripped away all the image buildup from his family of origin but truly needed to heal from the wounds they delivered. I pray he is well and connected with well people and a healthy community of faith that has allowed him to burst into freedom as he explores his passions.

Jeremiah 29:11 is a favorite verse of many. It is a verse I hold on to with promise and hope and also, as I have mentioned, the verse displayed in my home and at the entrance of The Lamb Center.

> "For I know the plans I have for you," declares
> the Lord, "plans to prosper you and not to harm
> you, plans to give you hope and a future."

What about you? Has God placed a desire deep within your heart? Has our Western culture or Christian image altered or enhanced your plan? Have your dreams of being a hairdresser, fashion designer, or a race car driver not seemed godly enough? Did a parent or loved one influence you toward a career, a pursuit, or even a place you should live?

Think about your early endeavors and dreams. Take some time to write out what you remember about your earliest visions and dreams and what you wanted to be when you grew up. How did you envision your home, and does it look anything like what you imagined? At what point in your life might you have exchanged a dream for a more manageable or pragmatic choice? Did someone influence that metamorphosis? Or did God Himself direct you?

Take some time to talk to God in a quiet place. Journey with Him into the heart of the matter. Listen to what He is asking you about your heart's desire. Listen to your own sacred heart and respond with the truth. Tell Him your dreams. Tell Him your disappointments. Mourn the loss of a dream. Most of us have them. Converse with God about what's on your heart and mind. Listen to Jeremiah 29:12–14:

> "Then you will call upon me and come and pray
> to me, and I will listen to you. You will seek me
> and find me when you seek me with all your
> heart. I will be found by you," declares the Lord,
> "and I will bring you back from captivity."

> "Be still before the Lord and wait patiently for
> him." (Psalm 37:7)

Cooperate with Him to uncover *your* heart's desires and His destiny for you. Strip away the expectations of others and listen to the call of God on your heart. When He was here on earth, Jesus said, "But the gateway to life is very narrow and the road is difficult, and only a few ever find it" (Matthew 7:14 NLT).

Never forget the *everything* promise (Romans 8:28). He *will* use everything. Yes, everything. The good, the bad, the ugly, the pain, the nonsense, the suffering, and even your hard-earned credentials and experiences. For your good and His glory. You can take that to the bank!

It's not too late to hit the reset button. As you lay your life down on the altar before Him, listen to His heart and your heart beating together. I AM will lead you into the desires, destiny, and calling He planned from the beginning of time. You can do amazing things. Together. Just *Imagine!*

Questions to Ponder:

1. Do you think Brian was careless or brave? Why?
2. Have you ever had the experience of receiving a physical gift instead of a human connection like Brian did? How did it make you feel? Share your story.
3. Have you as a child or as an adult experienced dream sabotage? Explain.
4. If you are a parent or guardian, are you tempted to get things "right" and shape the choices of your children? Is it because you didn't have choices as a child? Explain.
5. Some people have an experience with God and know their calling specifically. Others come upon it by some tragedy or through their own sin or suffering. Share with the group your experiences and what you define as a "calling."
6. What Christian dogma rubs you the wrong way? Did you find yourself agreeing with Brian's parents or do you find the stereotypes of certain churches upsetting? Support your opinions with Scripture.
7. Do you relate to any of the Bible characters mentioned in this chapter? Do you think they had an idea of the importance of their roles in history? Relate your life to a Bible story that seems like how your story is unfolding. Where are you in your story?

8. What are your leanings or strengths? Try not to over spiritualize these; be honest about what you wanted to be when you grew up. How does that match up with what you are doing in life right now?

9. Think of your worst choice. Through the lens of Romans 8:28, how might God see your choice?

10. Looking again at Romans 8:28, do you have a story in your life that has the privilege of hindsight being 20/20? Share it with the group.

11. After your time alone contemplating your calling, journal your thoughts. Share it with the group or with a trusted friend.

Interlude – Heart Check!

*A*s we have journeyed together into some deep stories, I hope you have looked differently at the homeless people you may have encountered while stopped at an intersection or walking down the street. Yes, they could have histories of bad choices, addictions, mental illness, abandonment, or trauma, but they are fellow human beings like you, with their own stories. I hope your stripped-down, less-covered-up self is starting to identify with your *own* soul needs *and* the needs of others. My prayer is that compassion and kindness for others, as well as yourself, has risen up in your soul and overflowed from your heart. That you have stopped covering up the truth about your story and have given God places in your heart you didn't even know were wounded. When God floods into the deepest wounds of us, we can better understand ourselves and others.

A few of the less obvious obstacles within the Christian experience, which keep us from moving forward into authenticity and living God's abundant life, are in the chapters ahead. They don't seem like roadblocks because most Christians wouldn't say they are obstacles. Each is complex and biblical. Each is tangled in Christian culture—and confusion. One is forgiveness. Another is judging. And the last is the body of Christ.

Join me in looking even deeper into our hearts as we take a candid and broad look at these important topics and the precision with which we need to obey the Spirit of God. The Lamb Center guests challenge me to look deeper into these essentials of the Christian walk with a fresh perspective. Held too tightly, they can be roadblocks to wholeness. Held up to the Light with a loose grip, we can discover more freedom than we ever imagined. This requires expert precision and direct Holy Spirit leading.

> "Lead me into truth and teach me, for you *are* the God of my salvation; On You I wait all the day." (Psalm 25:5 NKJV)

CHAPTER NINE

Karen's Brave Prayer
or <u>Daring Forgiveness</u>

*A*fter I was in a good rhythm with my now weekly gig of leading Bible study at The Lamb Center, I could tell I was growing and stretching in compassion for my new friends. It is always an adventure; I never know who will be there, what they will bring, or how the Holy Spirit will show up. I began arriving with a spring in my step. Cover-up off. Yes, I'd still prepare a lesson, but less so, with just a few questions and cross-references. Less like teaching and more like, "Holy Spirit, what are we doing today?" and "What will You teach me through others today?" The beautiful brokenness of others and myself was becoming a blessing. I was seeing and learning about restoration. Learning through others. And learning through the exploration of my own heart. Another God-appointed day at The Lamb Center introduced me to Karen and to my next steps forward in wellness.

I didn't know Karen well, but she was soft-spoken, kind, and a faithful attender of the Friday morning Bible study. When not at the study, she hung out in the front of the building smoking cigarettes, rarely talking to others. She was a loner. Maybe I was drawn to her because she was more like me than other guests. White. About my age. Nothing very different other than a reddish complexion, which told me she maybe drowned her sorrows from time to time a little more than I did.

I rarely called on her to read Scripture references because her soft voice always got swallowed up in the din of other discussions in the large common space. At the table, those who always had something to say usually drowned her out. But this day was different. Perhaps the Holy Spirit was answering a prayer for me. I had asked God to show me the next step in handling the wounds others delivered to me.

My question to the group was about cultivating a better prayer life. Around the table, there were a few helpful suggestions. And then, Karen spoke up with surety and conviction. Her answer surprised all of us; it was profound.

"Whenever I experience anger, usually about a particular bad thing that happened to me, I say out loud that I forgive *them* again and again." She told us that what *they* had done to her was terrible, horrific.

There are certain times at The Lamb Center table when time seems to freeze. This was one of them.

She went on. "It changed my life for the worse, so I get scared, a lot, especially at night." Her prayer life had become her sanctuary of protection. It didn't take me long to envision what might have happened to Karen. The gravity of her words kept me spellbound for her remedy.

"What I do," she said, "is say this phrase over and over, out loud, three times: 'Lord, *I* forgive them. Lord, I *forgive* them. Lord, I forgive *them*.' Afterward, I experience peace. Peace enough to fall asleep." This was her antidote for fear, anger, and resentment. To forgive. And repeat. Then repeat it again, until she experienced the peace she craved.

Forced Forgiveness

Her wisdom gave me pause. I'd known all about forgiveness. Especially as a young girl. My brother and I were Sunday school good and did all the "oughts." We were taught to say "I'm sorry," even when we weren't, and "I forgive you," even when we were still angry about a meanness or oversight.

I learned to say the words, but did they ever meet my heart? Were the words offered too immediately, absolving any harm to self as meaningless—making my heart needs less important than the absolution of others—then named "godliness"?

In turn, I taught my children all the goodness of "I'm sorry" and "I forgive you." I was always proud when I was complimented on how polite and gracious our young children were, like I'd won the Mother of the Year prize for teaching what to say when you don't really mean it!

I even taught them, after asking to be excused from the table after a meal, to say, "Thank you for the delicious meal" as they scampered to clear their plates.

As a particularly fussy eater, not finishing much of anything, my son would say with the most unconvincing look, nearly gagging on peas and carrots hidden under his napkin, "Thank you for the delicious meal, Mommy."

I would graciously reply, "You are welcome. Thank you for clearing your plate."

Oh my word! Gracious and polite liar! He hated every minute of many of those meals. I think I need to apologize for teaching them to lie through their teeth, denying every feeling of their spirits. Ah, motherhood. Well, thankfully the manners stuck. As an added benefit, the feelings of some awful cooks they have surely encountered over the years have been spared.

Clean Slates

Karen caused me to reflect on my personal Christian journey and my forgiveness practices. I was taught to focus on self and the ways I had "trespassed" against others. I kept a short list with God, confessing all the sin that came to mind. Jesus' death and resurrection are about personal forgiveness. This is essential for faith, to both acknowledge and confess our sin to receive Jesus' forgiveness and justification (just as if I never sinned). "For God made Christ, who never sinned, to be the offering for our sin, so that we could be made right with God through Christ" (2 Corinthians 5:21 NLT). This is the good news of the gospel. Most reading this have accepted this gift of eternal life from Him (if you are unsure or need clarification, see the Salvation Prayer in the Appendix). Our hearts well up with gratitude as we realize that all our short-comings, blatant sins, and mistakes are covered with the blood of Jesus. Amazingly, He chooses to remember them no more (Jeremiah 31:34). This is merciful grace. God's grace is sweet for our soul.

Nevertheless, it is a good habit in prayer to reflect on personal sin, like setting the slate clean before going into intercession. Put in churchy terms, it's those sins of com-mission and omission in contrition! Throughout my journey of faith, I'd offer forgiveness whenever asked, and I would move on quickly. I even prayed for my "enemies" (Matthew 5:44), even though I couldn't quite identify them as such, more like those who disappointed my expectations. Being a "nice" person doesn't lend itself to having many enemies; there is nothing to really fight. These were my religious and prayer practices as often as I remembered to do so.

Maybe like your church, the monthly communion ser-vice at our church offered both a silent time to reflect on personal sin and ask God for forgiveness and a beautifully scripted corporate prayer of confession to God (included in the Appendix). When doing both of those practices, I would reflect and inspect all I had done and not done that would disappoint God, which broke His heart and law. That was the extent of my forgiveness practices. Hold no grudges. Keep no record of wrong (1 Corinthians 13:5). Keep the slate clean. I rarely thought about sins that happened *to* me.

Rattle Some Cages

The Lord's Prayer, generally familiar and repeated the same way among all Christians, includes the important request "Forgive us our sins," evoking elements of both guilt and mercy (Matthew 6:12 NLT). Different denominations of the faith tend to lean heavily to one side or the other. A little more grace or a little more judgment. More love and compassion or more guilt and repentance. We forget, though, that the forgiveness line in the Lord's Prayer reads in full, "And forgive us our sins, *as* we forgive those who sin against us" (italics mine). There is the additional third element of examining the wrongs that have been committed *against* us.

When we walk through pain caused to us by the sins of others, we grapple with the reality that if Jesus died for *my* sins, He must have died for the sins of others too. And that must include the sins against me, even if those others aren't sorry or even aware of the pain they've caused. But we must not forget that God is very much aware of and cares deeply about what happened *to* us.

In my interactions with friends outside The Lamb Center, and those I meet at the long wooden table, I am often stunned by what I hear. Friends share stories of terrible sins committed against them like third-person reports instead of appropriate grief for their wounded souls. They say things like "It was so long ago," or "It was no big deal," or "It's been forgiven and forgotten," or worse yet, "I deserved it." A date rape with the threat of death if she screamed. An angry father backhanding a child in the face until her nose bled. A middle school boy put in an oxygen tent to recover from the violent push of an angry parent. An abusive verbal tirade of a spouse. A boy being made to dress like a girl by Christian camp counselors to make fun of how homesick he was. A young lady left with ongoing nightmares after an occult film was shown at a church sleepover event. A teenager in shock after a car accident told by nurses not to call her parents crying, lest they get into an accident of their own on the way to the hospital. All of these were reported to me with a near blasé or anecdotal tone.

The more whole I become, the more dumbfounded I am at how people, especially Christians, belittle their past and present harm as insignificant to their current reality. Clearly, the effects of the circumstances are still in play. Nothing has ever been done to help those parts of their damaged souls, as if God is only concerned with forgiveness and *not* justice and compassion.

With Christian culture urging us to forgive without considering the damage, we can see why so many people are the walking wounded, shutdown and not living life fully. Some continue to wound others because their own insensitive hearts have become callous to real harm. It is hard to have compassion for others when you have not even considered compassion for yourself.

The Nice Christian Lie / Life

I get it. Many of us are taught to never complain or mention the past or the harm done to us. We are told it is sinful to remember another's sin. We are to be grateful, count our blessings, and ignore or quickly forget the sins against us.

We are tempted to say, "Nothing bad ever happened to me" or "I had a perfect childhood." I offer that no one walks through this world unscathed. *No one*. And although some have had more tragic lives than others, "all have sinned and fall short of the glory of God" (Romans 3:23). That means that you and I have sinned against others *and* that you and I have been sinned against. It is an inevitability.

Dan Allender rather dramatically boils this down: "We are all murderers, thieves or adulterers."[1] All sin drills down to these big ones when you consider the motives, thoughts, and deeds. This includes your parents. And before you get smug enough to say, "Why yes, indeed it does," look in the mirror and say, "Me too."

Introspection

When inspecting the stories of harm in your own life, which include sins *against* you, it is important to be aware of a few common tendencies. If you lean more toward controlling others, blaming and resentment are likely the pattern. Forgiveness is likely sabotaged and ignored. However, if you lean toward codependency, minimizing or covering over infractions with explanations is the go-to choice. Forgiveness is barely meaningful when it is immediately and mindlessly offered.

A more common tendency among those who are taught a loving, polite Christian spirit is to empathize too much with the wounding person and less with your own heart. Yes, it is gracious and good to show compassion, but you must remember what happened to stop it from happening again.

Once you recognize these inclinations, you can finally tell the truth about harm done to you and call it what it is. You can safely think through strategies to set proper boundaries for yourself. You can begin to set a course for healing your wounds. If you keep forgiving without seeing a pattern, the pattern of harm repeats. You repeat what you don't resolve, on either side of this continuum. This is where forgiveness and forgetting need to part ways.

Name what happened when your heart was broken and a whole new understanding of yourself and the themes of your life comes together like a puzzle.

Taking a Closer Look

Let's take a closer look at the notion of "forgive and forget." We do see examples of redemptive forgiveness in Scripture. Take Joseph forgiving his brothers for selling him into slavery (Genesis 50:15–20). He forgives them, saying, "what they intended for evil, God worked together for good" (verse 20). But does he ever really trust them again? He takes quite a bit of time to test them, even going as far as to insist they bring back his youngest brother, Benjamin, which required a long journey (Genesis 43). Then he plants false evidence in their caravan to see how they will react (Genesis 44). This was a long and important process for Joseph—and a difficult test for his father, Isaac, and his brothers. He twice tests the truthfulness and obedience of his brothers before he offers forgiveness. I get it. These brothers mocked him, sold him into slavery, and were willing to let him die (Genesis 37:19–27). Forgiveness. Okay. But in order for Joseph to say, "Move in and let's be friends again," a few tests were necessary. Joseph was wise, Pharaoh's second-in-command. He was no doormat to more of the same. Yes, he settled his entire family in the land of Goshen and provided for them lavishly (Genesis 47), but we don't really learn if he trusted his brothers to then hang out with his young sons or take them on road trips alone in the Egyptian desert!

Because Nice Matters

When the kids were young, I hung a sign in the kitchen that said *Because Nice Matters*. The world sure does need to be nicer, though the sign was strategically meant for my husband and not necessarily the children. I hammered that nail in with all the malice I could—over my dinner table, dadgummit! "Take that," I muttered with my little passive-aggressive tirade. That my children needed to be part of a propaganda effort ... well, again, good manners and kindness stuck. And I'm authentically *sorry*, kids!

Years later, when the Holy Spirit healed my husband's mean streak in a rather dramatic way, my husband graciously told both me and the children, "I'm sorry," and he asked for our forgiveness. Through some tears, we genuinely answered back, "I forgive you," even though trusting and understanding this change would take years.

Forgiveness *is* the start of a process. You forgive as an act of obedience to God, as an act of your will. It *doesn't* mean a solving of all the complications and implications of the sin.

The Whole Story

We sin against others, and others sin against us. This is life and has been since the day of Adam and Eve's fall from grace in Genesis 3. Like them, we too are outside the Garden of Eden and are incapable of having perfect relationships, with God and others. That is why God sent His Son as the perfect sacrifice for us all (John 3:16). When we accept His gift of forgiveness, we step into a redemptive relationship with God. And in living out this new life with Christ, Jesus tells us to forgive others as He forgives us (Luke 11:4, Mark 11:25–26).

We are complex beings, made up of body, soul, spirit, heart, mind, *and* will. Once we forgive as an act of our will, we need to do some soul work. Our mind and heart need attention too! To forget the other elements is like cutting off your legs and trying to move forward. Our minds may replay the event over and over. Our hearts and spirits may wrestle with brokenness as God begins to make us well. Our emotions may range from anger to hurt to disappointment to disillusionment—and rightly so. We need to look at the full story. To give God the whole process, not just the obedience of forgiveness. We can bring all aspects of ourselves to God for justice, recompense, and healing. We become more whole in the process. It is more than simple obedience to God; it is an agreement to begin the process of healing, cooperation with God to melt the deadly chains of bondage traced all the way back to hell.

Breaking the Chains

Forgiveness melts the powerful chains that can keep us captive and separate us from God's best plan.

Forgiveness begins the process of melting the chains of bondage, sin & death

Romans 6:23; Romans 8:6

<u>Between You & the Sin</u> - transforms righteous anger into proper healing

Ephesians 4:26-27; 31-32

<u>Between Sin & the Sinner</u> - gives the sinner an opportunity to repent

Matthew 18:15-17; Luke 17:3-4

<u>Between You & the Sinner</u> - prevents bitterness; offers choices in relationship as you wisely follow God's direction - 1. restoration 2. reconciliation 3. relationship (none are guarantees)

Psalm 119:105-128; Galatians 5:22-26; 6:1-10; Hebrews 4:12-13; 15-16

<u>Between You, the Sinner & Enemy</u> - invites God's POWER to work it together for good

Genesis 50:20; Romans 8:28

<u>Between Power & Enemy</u> - foils evil plot; shows the world God's love

Romans 8:1-8

Figure #1

Figure #1 shows the chains that get established when someone sins against us. The follower of Christ who is the victim gets chained to another's sin. It affects us, whether we admit it or not.

When we forgive as an act of our will, we obey God. We trust Him to do what no person can do and cooperate with His plan of redemption. We hand God the mess to deal with instead of trying to clean it up on our own.

Forgiveness melts the chains between you and the sin and you and the sinner. This is when you and God can attend to the needs of your heart and mind and all the ways you have been affected, as we have already covered. Anger and resentment begin to dissolve. Bitterness dissipates as we look to God instead of the offending sinner to pay us back for the wrongdoing.

Forgiveness melts the chain between the sin and the sinner. It gives the sinner the opportunity to cooperate with God as well and move toward repentance. In cases where the sinner is still living, possibilities in the relationship open up. Restoration and reconciliation are possible. On the other hand, it may not be safe or realistic to enter into the same dynamic as before the sin occurred. Better boundaries may need to be established. You get to decide whether to be in relationship with the person or not and to what extent. It is clear relationship decisions require great wisdom from God.

Forgiveness melts the chains between you, the sinner, and the enemy. You let God transform what the enemy intended for harm into good (Genesis 50:20). In fact, Romans 8:28 promises God will work together *everything* for our good if we love Him and are called according to His purposes (if we have accepted Jesus Christ as our personal Savior).

Now for the really exciting part! This process of forgiveness melts the chains between power and the enemy. You take the power the enemy was trying to exact upon your life and hand it back to God. The enemy tries to "steal, kill and destroy" you through others, but God has already defeated the foe and promised abundant life (John 10:10).

With God, you get to foil the plots and dismantle the effects of the enemy, both for you and for the person who sinned against you. You get to deal the adversary another blow when you remove his power from your domain. Anyone feel like they are in the *Matrix* films now? This is the wonder-working power of grace. You can declare, "This is God's territory." The enemy and his minions can go straight to hell, where they belong.

You get to exhibit the love of God to a retaliatory world (Romans 8:1–8). Authentic forgiveness is counterintuitive. It's countercultural. It is God's way, so He demonstrated with His own Son, Jesus, and forgave us first. A taste of undeserved kindness and the melting of many chains—the chains of death (Romans 6:23).

Community Effect

In the summer of 2015, horrific murders *in* a church took place in the peaceful town of Charleston, South Carolina. The incident was named the "Charleston Nine" so as not to give name and fame to the murderer but rather the victims. Honestly, I think God got the credit in this forgiveness scenario. The victims' families were nearly immediate in their expressions of forgiveness toward the murderer. Perhaps it was what the Bible study, interrupted by the murderer, was about that day. Regardless, it was an amazing feat featured on the evening news, which seemed even more the story than the catastrophe. Forgiveness made the news! In fact, the name of the church is Emmanuel (God with us). There are so many reports about evil nowadays, airing twenty-four hours a day worldwide, with more frequency to those of Christian faith. This forgiveness and love seemed to settle down the charming town of Charleston, delivering peace during the anguish. God was there. He was given the power over this town by obedient Christians in the face of evil. The Church stood strong and beautiful as it was featured over and over again, its cross standing tall.

The opposite effect of unforgiveness plays out in crimes and further aggravation in cities like Chicago, where murder leads to more murder and vengeance seems a way of life for some people. The Charleston story of forgiveness stopped the nonsense of evil. Forgiveness has divine qualities of healing communities as well as individuals.

But did those forgiving Christians in Charleston invite the murderer into their homes for dinner that night or protect him from punishment? Did they enter into a relationship with him? Certainly not. Thankfully, they forgave him and let justice be served.

Extremes and Seventy Times Seven

Biblical wisdom tells us most things are permissible in moderation. Extremes of eating are a perfect example. Gluttony leads to obesity, and too little food leads to starvation. The happy medium is the ticket to good health.

In the book of Matthew, Peter asks Jesus, "How often should I forgive someone who sins against me? Seven times?" (which is more than the Jewish letter of the law, three times). "'No, not seven times,' Jesus replied, 'but seventy times seven'" (Matthew 18:21–22 NLT). The number seven in Scripture suggests perfection, something complete. Like with many doctrines and Scriptures, Christians take just that one segment of Scripture and tether their lives to the precise answer. The takeaway is that we keep tolerating whatever comes our way and just "forgive and forget," like our personal boundaries and self-worth need to be tossed out with the trash. We assume good Christian living includes a well-worn doormat to harm. "Turn the other cheek" (another of Jesus' teachings in Matthew 5:39) and move along, disregarding emotional health.

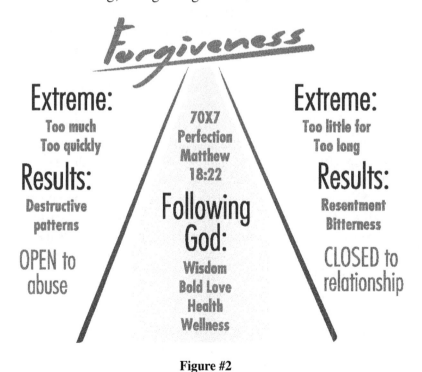

Figure #2

Figure #2 shows the extremes in forgiveness. Forgiving too much, too quickly, without inspection is dangerous. When we do that, we don't analyze destructive and repetitive patterns in our relationships. This leaves us open to patterns of abuse, sometimes for generations.

The other extreme takes another teaching of Jesus from the book of Luke: "If your brother sins *and* disregards God's precepts, solemnly warn him; and if he repents *and* changes, forgive him" (Luke 17:3 AMP). This holds that only a repentant and changed believer should be forgiven. Remember, the definition of Christian repentance suggests that the sinner changes his mind, turns around, and doesn't repeat the sin. Maybe Jesus was teaching Peter and us much more than mathematics. He was teaching us common sense.

However, taking that biblical text alone and holding it too tightly leaves us open to the other extreme. The forgiving too little for too long is the perfect recipe for an ulcer and bad health. That kind of "remembering" is called a grudge. Bitterness and resentment are the keys to an early heart attack and a life of misery. We lock ourselves in a canister of analysis of folks' repentance and rot, closing ourselves off to healthy relationships. We are closed off to community when we spend time looking at others' sins and their attitudes before we budge. The passage about removing the plank from our own eye before dealing with the splinter in another's eye speaks to this extreme (Matthew 7:5).

Most of us have never taken the time to analyze what Jesus really meant in entirety. Luke 17:4 repeats the idea to continue forgiving a *repentant* sinner as often as he repeats the sin. Again, the biblical definition would suggest the sin would *not* be repeated if there was truly repentance.

I maintain what Jesus meant by the "seventy times seven" (or perfection) is just that—perfection. There is wisdom and discernment between the two extremes. As we follow God, we love others boldly in the truth of real forgiveness, embracing health and wellness in our relationships.

More Than a Benefit

The perceived "benefit" from either of those extremes is also a factor.

Christians often pair "forgive and forget" with the lack of angst over grudges. Our hearts feel better when they are lighter. That is true and right—unless you are forgiving something that is harming you (abuse, for example). Feeling better shouldn't be the motivation for forgiving, but it *is* a benefit to our soul. Sometimes, we want the quick relief of "everything's okay" instead of the real, long-lasting change God desires.

On the other side, those who saw one parent abuse another and swore they would never tolerate such a situation might say, "I refuse to let *anyone* harm me." That "protection" is their perceived benefit. They hold forgiveness under lock and key and end up in the venomous place of unforgiveness and bitterness, closed off to any relationship.

You see, friends? Wisdom is needed here. James 1:5 says when we ask God for wisdom, He will give it generously.

Wisdom is the perfection. Discernment is the key.

Wisdom and Recognition

Even though my husband had apologized for his long pattern of behavior years earlier, I still had some work to do. He felt relieved by my forgiveness, but I was still reeling. First, I had to recognize the pattern of emotional abuse in my home as *sin* against me. Only then, and with the harness of wise boundaries established, could authentic forgiveness take place. Through counseling, I'd learned to alter my responses and actions, which forced needed changes to my husband's behavior. Indeed, this was what got him to acknowledge something wasn't working in the first place. To continue to ignore the problem by saying it was okay was *not* godly forgiveness. It was unwise and unsafe.

It took me a long time to realize that my quick "forgiveness" at every instance of unkindness, without consideration to myself or children (motivated by my desire for "peace" more than wellness) was not authentic forgiveness at all. It was a toxic delay to a growing problem. Years later, my husband said each time I "forgave" so quickly, he ended up hating himself even more. It did *not* invite him into repentance but unbeknownst to me into a shame-based hatred of himself.

Biblically, I learned the ones Jesus said are "blessed" (in the Beatitudes) were the peace*makers,* not the peace*keepers* (Matthew 5:9). What I was perpetuating was a toxic form of cover-up. I was covering up the problem; I wasn't helping myself, my husband, or my children.

The research I did about emotional abuse gave me great understanding and compassion for my husband. I learned about the deep-seated insecurity and self-loathing that causes someone to manipulate and control other loved ones. The abuser needs to live vicariously through others' actions, and reactions, because of the deep need in his or her own soul. The melted chains of authentic forgiveness detached my husband from his sin. I hated the sin in my home, but I had compassion for this wounded, wounding man.

My forgiveness shifted things. Though I learned hurt people hurt people, I also learned hurt from someone else causes damage to the trust and love "muscle." Alas, entrenched patterns are quite difficult to undo. There is residue and fallout. Godly wisdom, *not* an answer that looks good and makes other church friends smile, is needed when discerning the next steps for a relationship after forgiveness is in place.

These few short paragraphs took years in real life. Much soul-searching and many decisions a normal "church girl" wouldn't make. The Christian culture in me wanted everything to be "textbook" and "all's well that ends well." I wanted my family's story to be featured on the next *Focus on the Family* broadcast. I wanted to skip hand in hand with my husband into a sunset of forgiveness, with our children following, amazed with God's goodness. But God's answers usually don't follow the fairytale narratives we place in our answered prayer categories.

I changed. God did give me wisdom. I realized a real wakeup call was needed after my cries for marriage counseling and therapy were met with not only "no" but "never." My heart, broken all over again, went cold. It would take a break in the relationship before substantial changes came to the husband I'd forgiven.

God knew forgiveness would set us both free from the captor and bring us closer to Him for authentic, individual healing. But it certainly didn't look like what Christian culture would tell me it should. Christian culture would suggest that because I'd forgiven my husband and he'd changed we were good to go. It all looked good enough on the outside. We were ready to lead the new couple's ministry. Not. It took and is still taking work to heal old wounds and patterns developed from those old sins done against me.

From Ankle Bracelets to Charms

Since my emotional journey into authentic wholeness started some ten years ago now, I have worn symbolic jewelry. A little Old Testament meets strip mall, I know. But it's my way of making an altar to the Lord for what He has done for me. They are things (usually simple) that signify milestones and cause me to remember "God taught me this." I rarely share them with others. However, if someone ever compliments me on one of those special pieces of jewelry, I usually explain the significance (they can be great conversation starters into deeper things).

At a homeless day shelter, I'm careful to wear less jewelry. I don't want to be showy or act like I have all the things when folks are there with only the clothes on their backs.

One piece was given to me by my friend Judy. It's simple, a silver bracelet with a tiny dangling cross. Judy's friend had given it to her because she admired Judy's faithfulness and courage, how she walked with grace and forgave some things that quite frankly most people wouldn't.

Judy, in turn, said she admired my faith walk. She saw my courage and how I walked with grace, forgave, and forged ahead with authenticity when I didn't know exactly where that would land me. I wore it proudly knowing I was following God in some unknown places, where faith grows in lonely petri dishes.

The last day I saw Karen, she was out in the front parking lot of The Lamb Center smoking a cigarette. It was a sunny day after Bible study. She waved and thanked me for the lesson. As I walked toward her, I sensed God tugging at my wrist!

Tears brimming, I took off the little cross bracelet and gave it to Karen. She was overwhelmed, nearly dropping her cigarette with surprise. I assisted with the presentation and placed it on her wrist. I told her I was proud of her faith walk. I was inspired by her forgiveness of the unforgivable. I affirmed my admiration of her courage. I wanted her to own a symbol of her faithfulness.

Future

Although I haven't seen Karen since, I hope and pray her faithfulness and courage have brought her housing and a new life, one fear doesn't dim. I pray God has blessed her for willingly offering, "*I* forgive them. I *forgive* them. I forgive *them*." I pray she has learned the next steps in the process of forgiveness, which will bring her true wellness and the peace she so desperately seeks.

Precious friend, what forgiveness is needed in your journey of life? Is it one to ask for or one to give? Are you ready to look at how the sins done against you have affected you? Have you forgiven as an act of your will but not yet brought your mind and emotions to our wonderful Counselor? Are you ready to break the power of patterns and themes of generational sin in your lineage, restore hope in your community, or break through destructive patterns in your personal life? Power, freedom, and healing await your decision to start the process.

Questions to Ponder:

1. Imagine yourself in the Bible study at The Lamb Center. What advice would you offer about cultivating a better prayer life?

2. Have you ever forgiven someone who was unrepentant? What were the results? How did you experience peace? Explain.

3. What are your practices in dealing with your sins with God? What are your rituals or practices, both personally and in your church setting, in dealing with sin?

4. Have you ever tuned in to "forgive *as* you have been forgiven" in the Lord's Prayer? What do you think that really means? What does this look like in your life?

5. Give an example when you might have heard a loved one mention a sin committed against him or her in a rather matter-of-fact way. How did you respond?

6. How do you react to Dan Allender's assessment that we are all murderers, thieves, or adulterers?

7. Discuss some patterns or themes of sin in your life. Some you have committed repeatedly.

8. Explore the story of Joseph from the lens of forgiveness. Have a hardy discussion about how much he forgave and blessed others.

9. Do you believe we should forgive and *forget*? Have you ever put those two words together? Is remembering more like a grudge or is it healthy? Explain the balance.

10. What do you think of the saying "Because nice matters"? Are you one of those nice people? Have you had an experience with someone taking advantage of your niceness that may need proper boundaries? Describe it.

11. Discuss the matter of the will regarding forgiveness. Explain some soul work you had to do after forgiving someone. How did God help you move forward in wholeness?

12. Which link in the chain of forgiveness stood out to you? Think of a particular forgiveness scenario in your life. What aspect of that chain needs to be melted?

13. Are you a "walled-off" person who doesn't let others get too close? Or do you consider yourself a forgiving and kind person who is a bit of a doormat? How do you find the balance?

14. Talk about generational sins in your family. How did they affect you? What about your children? What actions could you take or have you taken to stop them from moving into the next generation?

15. Do you have any markers or symbols between you and God for times of growth and significance? Share and, if possible, show.

CHAPTER TEN

Nudge from the Judge or DeeAnn and Dave's Discernment

"*B*aloney, sir!" says the ubiquitous Judge Judy, "I don't care what you *think*! I'm the one who has to make a determination about what is fair." For years, we listened to this television personality with delight as she executed common sense judgments to outwardly ridiculous cases. Wouldn't it be great if it was as easy as she made it seem?

In truth, everyone must judge many things—information, people, and ideas. To live the abundant, adventurous, and purposeful life God has for us with Him, we must be able to make wise and sound judgments. These are different from snap judgments or a judgmental attitude based on self-righteous pride or cultural norms (including Christian culture). These *sound* judgments are formed with truth and wisdom.

Merriam-Webster, ever solid definer of words, defines judging as "forming an opinion or conclusion about something."[1] But judgment is often complicated by other influences and distractions. And they seem to increase as the years go by. There is so much data and noise, so many opinions, about nearly everything, God included. Much of it is simply garbage. Even our news, which we turn to in order to understand the world around us, has become about views. On top of that, societal norms warn us not to judge anything.

Families of origin may play a strong, but wrong, influence. Christian culture can encourage us to listen to others instead of the still, small Voice within. It is imperative we wade through all this muck and understand what judgment is and what it is not so we can make choices wisely. This includes practical decisions on our path (more like a swift-flowing river) of life. If I had understood and exercised sound judgment, it would have saved me years of heartache and angst.

The Ultimate Judge

The place to start in any discussion about judging is God Himself. He is the ultimate Judge and will judge all human beings on judgment day (Revelation 20). Jesus says in Matthew 12:36–37, all "must give account on judgment day for every idle word you speak. The words you say will either acquit you or condemn you" (NLT). He will bring "our darkest secrets to light and will reveal our private motives. Then God will give to each one whatever praise is due" (1 Corinthians 4:5 NLT). Jesus continues the theme of judging in John 5:30: "I can do nothing on my own. I judge as God tells me. Therefore, my judgment is just, because I carry out the will of the one who sent me, not my own will" (NLT).

Throughout the Bible we get many pictures of the wrath of God, even His wrath toward those within His sanctuary. In Ezekiel 9, God speaks to Ezekiel through a vision about judgment in Jerusalem. He directs the harsh judgment to be unleashed, starting with those in charge of His own temple. He is extremely severe toward *anyone* who maligns His temple. Since Pentecost, the Holy Spirit resides in believers; *we* are now temples of God (1 Corinthians 3:16). So those who harm other believers, particularly those in shepherding roles within the church, are under God's severe judgment. In fact, He says anyone who causes one of His little ones to stumble would be better off tying a millstone around his neck and drowning in the sea (Matthew 18:6). And like Ezekiel 9, 1 Peter 4:17 warns us, "it is time for judgment to begin with God's household." We are held to a high standard.

Those who receive Christ Jesus as Lord of their lives are to follow the Spirit of Truth into all the truth (John 16:13). Part of that is wisely discerning the bad fruit of certain people, whom He describes as wolves in sheep's clothing (Matthew 7:15–18). Furthermore, as God's children, we must investigate and uncover deeds of darkness, especially within the Church. His written Word says we are to, "Carefully determine what pleases the Lord. Take no part in the worthless deeds of evil and darkness; instead expose them" (Ephesians 5:10–11 NLT). It sounds like we need sound judgment now more than ever!

We ignore this topic at our own peril. Not understanding the truth about proper judgment, the way God designed it, nearly derailed my purpose and path of life. Similarly, you can likely remember when you desperately needed God-directed wisdom and discernment but had it derailed by listening to the outside racket. As we endeavor to find our truest selves, devoid of image, and press in to know more of God, let's take a broad look at how this important and biblical concept can transform our walks of faith. Your destiny hangs in the balance.

Nudged

One Friday morning at the Bible study around the large wooden table, we went around introducing ourselves, as I noted we had some newcomers. One man, Assad, shared that it was his first day at The Lamb Center in seven years.

His story came out later while we were exploring Galatians. We were discussing how our spheres of influence, like Paul's, were being used by God. Assad chimed in cheerfully with his testimony. He had come to The Lamb Center that day only to thank "a guy named Dave" for showing him Christian kindness seven years ago. Laughter ensued when Assad described him physically and then asked, "Does anyone here know a guy named Dave?" Of course, *everyone* knows Dave at The Lamb Center!

As I have mentioned before, Dave's presence at The Lamb Center is authentic and caring. He courageously shares his past mistakes, his addiction, and all his bad decisions cost him. He likes to say that his first encounter with The Lamb Center was brought about by a "nudge from the judge." He had to do community service hours for something that occurred because of his poor choices in relation to alcohol. As God prodded Dave's heart, he was moved by a tough-loving and persistent sponsor in AA and the authentic souls around the old wooden table of The Lamb Center, who all led him deep into the heart of the matter. God's pursuit of Dave through others was irresistible. Now, as director, Dave's brokenness, his gifts, and his real life join his real faith for a story that draws others into community—and to the foot of the cross.

Unfortunately, that day Dave was away at a conference. Maybe it was because God didn't want him overwhelmed with blushing, as his private selflessness, wise discernment, and humble leadership were on display for us all to admire.

The Real Deal

Assad's story was gripping. He too had struggled with an addiction, brought on by his only son's suicide. After his addictions led to a crime, at that time a Muslim, he went to his mosque for direction and help. Instead of offering understanding and compassion, though, they called the police and banned him from the community forever. He had "shamed" their faith by his addictions and actions. From there, he landed at The Lamb Center while he awaited a court hearing. Because Assad had no community, family, or friends to help him even get to the court appearance, Dave bought him a suit and tie and drove him to the courthouse where he was to appear before the judge for sentencing.

Dave never once mentioned Jesus but clearly showed His love to an unrepentant but lost sinner, still reeling from rejection, which added to his anger and grief. While Dave respected the law and justice of the court appearance, he exhibited mercy, much like God did through the sacrifice of Jesus. Assad was sentenced to seven years. While sobering up in prison, the voice of his own son spoke to him in a dream, saying, "What are you doing with your life, Father?" This supernatural experience scared him into the arms of a discerning prison chaplain, who formally introduced him to Jesus, the Savior.

And so, seven *long* years later, Assad was there at The Lamb Center to thank Dave for sharing the love that had drawn him in. In this authentic community around the table, he confessed and professed his faith in Christ that now held him together. He passionately pleaded with anyone who would listen to "follow Jesus while you have the chance." He begged all around him not to cover up their pain with addiction or crime. With wisdom, he called us to "go there—to the heart of the matter, before you waste precious years like I did."

On this day, his testimony, bright and beautiful, was especially helpful to another guest. Nadim, also Muslim, was at The Lamb Center doing community service for a lesser crime than Assad's. While Nadim explored the Christian faith at Bible study that day, Assad's timely testimony magnified Christ's love and made it tangible in a way only God could design. This unrehearsed and powerful preaching from a broken life living in authentic community was exactly what we all needed to hear. *This* is the body of Christ. This is community, where the deepest wounds shared in authenticity and humility, show us the real heart of the matter. This is where God wants to go in each of us and in us as a community. The revealing of the whole truth in an environment led by the Truth is impactful and irresistible.

Now, if I had made snap judgments on outside appearances or quieted Assad because I had not authorized his statement or theology, this story would have stayed hidden. Had I stuck to a rigid outline of events or taught like a heavy-handed authority instead of wisely following God's lead and allowing others to share, this powerful teaching would have been silenced. Because I nudged my own judgmental attitude out of the way, what God did in us, through us, and with us was explosive!

After that, thirsty for more understanding, I decided to explore the different kinds of judgment more carefully. What I discovered changed my life.

Friendly Fire

Although in John 7:24, Jesus tells us "not to judge by appearance [superficially and arrogantly], but to judge fairly *and* righteously" (AMP), Christians seem to take aim at their own with particular delight. The body of Christ can be brutal in quick judgment of other servants in the public arena, causing confusion inside and outside the Christian community. Like a rodeo, other Christians blindly jump on the bandwagon for a Wild West beatdown of anyone outside the Christian culture box. Like with The Lamb Center Bible study group, I implore brothers and sisters to read, listen, and think for themselves with wisdom and Holy Spirit leading before they tear down other gifted teachers and pioneers (James 4:11–12). Had Ananias listened to his friends in the faith who discouraged him from heading to Damascus to talk to the newly transformed Paul (Acts 9:10–16), we may never have had most parts of the New Testament.

Let's face it, most converts to the Christian faith are not wooed by theologians waxing eloquently about the split hairs of doctrine. Although we need to be careful about false teaching and protect sound doctrine, we need to remember the impact of what may bring outsiders into faith in Christ. Being right doesn't always translate as compassion to the timid seeker. It's a turnoff. An arctic blast of air in the face of someone drawing closer for a quiet look at the warmth of Jesus.

Think of your own story. What drew you into an interest in Jesus? Was it a piece of art? A book that placed a question in your soul? Was it a story of another person wrestling with truth? Was it listening to your own heartbeat in a yoga class? Was it a sunset or nature that drew you into the beauty of God? Or the sweet love of your loyal golden retriever when you went through a divorce? Or a hail Mary prayer for healing even though you weren't sure you believed? Or maybe like Assad, you had someone like Dave offer an act of kindness when no one else would. Or maybe you had an impactful dream that rattled you to your core.

Just imagine a hammer in the hands of a "well-meaning" Christian telling you that book is inappropriate. Or you shouldn't worship nature. Or yoga is New Age nonsense. Or a fictional story isn't theologically correct. Or dogs don't go to heaven. Or God doesn't listen to the prayers of non-Christians. Or you should stay away from those crazy Muslims. Or God doesn't speak through dreams anymore. The embers of faith are fragile. Quick, cunning responses and snap judgments uttered with all-knowing pride can quickly destroy what God was exciting in a human heart.

We are to work *with* God and do all He planned for us to do (Ephesians 2:10). God will bring all our efforts to light; His fire will test the quality of each man's work. If it survives, that individual will receive his reward. If it is burned up, he will suffer loss; he himself will be saved, but only as one escaping through the flames (1 Corinthians 3:12–15). God alone is the Judge of a person's work.

Romans 12:1–3 encourages us not to be conformed to the patterns of this world, but to be transformed by the *renewing* of our minds. Stay fresh to the ways God might be inspiring others and infusing your own mind with truth. *Imagine* all that can be accomplished on this earth as each of us lives out our unique destiny. We can encourage and cheer others on in doing the same! My experiences at The Lamb Center opened up my eyes to all the wonderful things I AM is doing with and through a myriad of believers with different backgrounds, gifts, and talents.

Sober Judgment

I must admit, those recovering addicts like Dave and Assad around the table are the absolute best. Those who have been through a twelve-step program are real and raw, through and through. They spot a cover-up liar a mile away and an imposter pride monger from further away. I have learned to keep the recovering alcoholics close by as my "BS meters" (from which I am not exempt!) at Bible study. They have gone deep into their souls and stripped away image and all the baloney. They tell the truth about themselves and others. You never hear an addict say to someone struggling, "*What?* How did you get yourself into *that* situation?"

At one of the Bible studies, Dave's phone went off. It was another recovering addict who had fallen "off the wagon." Dave stepped away to console and encourage this wavering and shame-filled sister. Then, he came back to the table with the news. We stopped everything and prayed for this dear, real sister struggling in the battle.

During another study, in the middle of a discussion about temptation, a lady's phone chirped. It was her ex-dealer wanting to know where she'd been and if she needed another "fix." Again, stripped of judgmental attitudes, we stopped everything and went to God. By linking arms of faith, we joined her in battle to strengthen embers of faith and courage.

When we tell the truth about our own situations, we can more easily listen without contemptuous judgment or disdain, but with acceptance and wisdom. That said, addicts' tough-love approach to *anything* that might derail their sobriety is the "essential" to their "faith" in the recovery process. Proper and wise judgment are necessary as they lean on each other in the community of recovery, much like the body of Christ should operate.

Because I attended an AA meeting at The Lamb Center with a friend's daughter who needed courage, I experienced firsthand their fellowship of *real*. Ironically, the group was on the seventh step that day: humility. Although a facilitator leads the group, there is no hierarchy, just camaraderie. No one is judging each other, but instead, all are willing to go to the deep in each other's stories. They support and encourage each other on to success.

Sadly, the young woman I brought never returned to AA. The trappings of The Lamb Center scared her. She said she was frightened by all the "crazy people with problems." Unless we see ourselves humbly, just like the "wretched, miserable, poor, blind and naked" (Revelation 3:17), we cannot see the problem behind all the cover-up. No authentic community exists that doesn't own *both* the depravity *and* the sanctity of other human life. We all need Jesus in every nook and cranny of our broken lives.

My Depravity and Sanctity

Although I began to experience freedom at The Lamb Center and walk in step with God to avoid making snap judgments about people and His leading, I didn't have as much clarity when I walked back into my own home and heart. Instead of listening for God's leadership and voice, I listened to every "authority" on earth, from sermons, to books, to people's dogma about certain Scripture references and even to others' similar stories. It seemed everyone had exact answers, but no one else was DeeAnn, with my exact situation and questions. I had not yet learned about the other kind of judging—the good kind— that, in step with the flow of God, would allow me to make sound judgments and decisions in my own life. Most of my few soul friends who knew my story were growing weary of my indecision. My mind was a ping pong match, exhausted by my own lack of direction and decisive action. It's as if the message "don't judge" lingered in the back of my mind.

Don't Judge

Is anyone else tired of hearing "don't judge" whenever you state an opinion about a behavior or untruth, especially if it is firmly denounced by God in His written Word? Heck, you can barely say the sky is blue and the grass is green without back-lash! With Judge Judy, I say, "Do I have *stupid* stamped across my forehead?" Sadly, it seems the only views that are unacceptable in our society are Christian absolutes.

Believers can come under this same "don't judge" blanket statement and grow confused. I certainly did. But we *are* to make judgments. As we throw out the bathwater (judgmental attitudes, snap judgments), let us make sure we don't also throw out the baby (sound judgment), so to speak. Sound judgment is from God.

Let's look at what God says about executing sound judgment in our confusing world. Some of the texts are about judgment within the community of faith, and others are about unbelievers. As always, we can look to Jesus as an example of how He treated outsiders and His own followers. Those who fouled up His truth and temple were called out strongly (Matthew 21:12). He also had harsh words for those in authority who were burdening worshippers (as mentioned before). Some troublemakers and false inquiries were simply given the silent treatment (Matthew 26:63). No need to cast pearls before swine (Matthew 7:6). Serious seekers of truth, though, were always invited into conversation (Mark 10:17–31). Jesus assessed each situation. With the mind of Christ and total reliance on Him, we are to assess each situation too. As we go out into this perilous world, we are to be "wise as a serpents, and innocent as doves [have no self-serving agenda]" (Matthew 10:16 AMP).

Jesus, in the Sermon on the Mount, had quite a bit to say about making sound judgments about others. In Matthew 7:1–6 and in Luke 6:37–45, He doesn't say not to judge, but not to do so with an attitude of superiority or contempt. He says the same measure will be used back on us. He also wisely teaches that we best judge our own shortcomings first before attempting to correct or judge the issues in someone else's life. Keep your magnifying mirror handy (*not* to admire your image but to examine your own attitudes and actions) before you launch an inspection of others.

Only after we remove the "plank" from our own eye can we help our fellow believer get the "splinter" out of her eye. If you had a splinter in your eye, you would likely *invite* someone to help you get it out. But you wouldn't pick someone holding a sledgehammer or even a pointy tweezer. You would choose someone gentle and loving.

Ever open up to someone about a struggle, seeking advice, only to hear chapter and verse answers of a sledgehammer? Or ever had someone heap shame on you, suggesting it was your fault or sin that might have caused your pain? Or ever heard you shouldn't be sad or mad because others have it far worse than you do? It takes *wise* judgment to know with which Christians we are safe to share our hearts. Someone who has done work on their own soul can be trusted to help with a "splinter" or some needed discernment for the problems of life.

Jesus also asserts that we should not waste our time, effort, or wisdom on those who will trample the truth and "tear [us] to pieces" (Matthew 7:6). That, in and of itself, requires sound judgment to decipher who is seeking and who is just mocking the faith. Many of you have no doubt experienced the "tear you to pieces" when you (like me) have unwisely engaged a hostile unbeliever on Facebook with the truth of Scripture. We see the wisdom of discernment in Scripture for our everyday lives. These aren't cut-and-dried answers; they take nuanced judgment, wisdom, and maturity.

Thank God (literally) for the Holy Spirit, who gives us discernment when we tune in to His power and insight. Paul explains the necessity of relying on the Holy Spirit to handle each situation (1 Corinthians 2:12–16; 1 Corinthians 5:9–13). We need to realize that although most humans have basic common sense, common courtesy, and common grace (although these seem to be disappearing in our hostile world), unbelievers are not able to understand spiritual things without the Spirit of God. So, Paul asserts we are *not* to judge the people outside the body of Christ with the same measure! Certainly crimes and sin are to be dealt with and exposed, but the people are God's to handle.

However, we *are* to judge whom to challenge and with whom to associate in the body of Christ. Paul perfectly demonstrates wisdom in his approach toward Peter when challenging his tactics in Galatia (Galatians 2:11–21). The Proverbs are filled with wisdom and insight saying we *are* to "Speak up and judge fairly; defend the rights of the poor and needy" (Proverbs 31:9).

Making Judgments *for* God

Often, we allow our church *culture* to define exactly what God would do about difficult and complex situations, without asking Him what He says is just. We see throughout Scripture that He handles each situation differently, not in a formulaic way. Romans 3:4 says, "Let God be true and every man a liar. As it is written, 'so that you may be proved right when you speak and prevail when you judge.'" We need to go to God Himself for everything, not to what people say about Him and His judgments. There is a difference.

How many times have we judged a situation *for* God? By doing so, we run the risk of redefining I AM. Instead, we can ask the living, still speaking I AM. We can lay everything out before Him, then listen and look for His instructions. When we invite all of I AM into *all* of our heart and spirit, we begin to know more of *His* heart and *His* Spirit. In the same way that we strip off Christian image, we must also strip off any false image of who God is. When we do this, we get to know how He operates and what He thinks. We learn more intimately His justice and direction. We learn to look, see, and evaluate each situation and follow His lead. Then, we experience the brilliant truth of Romans 8:14: "For all who are led by the Spirit of God are the children of God."

1 Corinthians 2:10–12 says, "But it was to us that God revealed things by His Spirit. For His Spirit searches out *everything* and shows us God's deep secrets. No one can know a person's thoughts except that person's own spirit, and no one can know God's thoughts except God's own Spirit. And we have received God's Spirit (not the world's spirit), so we can know the wonderful things God has freely given us" (NLT; emphasis mine). God will lead!

Down River, DeeAnn

As I write this, "down river" from where I began in Chapter One, I look out over the tranquil and scenic Shenandoah River. During this summer getaway to experience communion with God, I have an opportunity to remember my path, or river of life, with its drop-offs, curves, ups and downs, constant movement, and undercurrents. Still, the river keeps on flowing. With my image stripped off, particularly in sharing my true story, I can see when I too heavily judged others' stories without being in their canoes! Or when I should have offered an oar of relief or a life jacket instead of judging how they got into that "stupid" predicament.

This season also gives me a time of thanks for those precious saints and nonbelievers alike who didn't make snap judgments about me but encouraged me to keep paddling. They didn't hit me over the head with the safety video I should have watched or correct my form, but rather came alongside me to shout a "Paddle harder left. Attagirl!" when my judgment was perhaps not sound. They didn't say "go for it" when there were dangerous rocks or a cliff up ahead. Instead, they warned me about the rapids and promised to come alongside me. Their well-timed responses were just what was needed to get me through the rocks with fewer scrapes and bruises. As I watch the river flow, I find it fascinating that the Shenandoah is one of a minority of rivers in the world that flow north.

Just as the Shenandoah flows in an unusual direction, the wise judgment I learned to execute in my home was *not* part of the usual Christian culture. In fact, it was against everything I was taught in church and in my family of origin. Yet, it was the *one* thing that broke the log jam in my river of life.

"I would *never* leave someone in abuse. That's not Me!" God said when I was at my wits' end with my marriage, having hunted down every remedy with little success or breakthrough. God expressed His anger at all injustice (Psalm 11:4–7). Pat answers and blanket statements were what most Christian folks declared. Christian culture seemed to show more interest in dogma than in my particular situation. But God showed me that part of making sound judgments is calling things for what they are and holding people accountable for their choices. God gave the decree of divorce in the Mosaic law to help women stuck in situations where they were uncared for or abused (Exodus 21:10). It's interesting how its origin of provision for the woman's welfare *isn't* explored in Christian culture, just that God *hates* divorce (Malachi 2:16), which is true. However, it doesn't say God hates *people* who divorce. And honestly, who *doesn't* hate divorce?

After drinking from a virtual fire hydrant of Christian opinions, I finally drank from God's fountain of truth and followed *His* lead. I met with lawyers. Some showed judgment that was callous and calculating, giving me manipulative control over the situation. I rejected them. God doesn't control people; He honors people's choices. I was not seeking retribution through manipulation. Then, I met an attorney whose compassion for justice was redemptive and collaborative. God and I liked that. I was seen, heard, and understood.

As "un-Christian" as it seems, God was leading me to end my marriage. As I prayed, I leaned into God for every word (literally) I needed to speak toward my husband. God just kept showing me His love and blank comic strip bubbles. "DeeAnn, I will fill in the blanks to show you *exactly* what to say." Unbeknownst to me, my husband was praying too. *He* was asking God for humility.

On a Wednesday morning, after a beautiful dream that reassured me of God's love, I went downstairs to begin my regular routine. As I poured my coffee, I purposely let the "walking on eggshells" feeling with my husband remain as he entered the kitchen. I left the emotional "mess" on the floor and did *not* pick it all up and fix the brokenness. He spoke first. "I feel a bit like our church with you, DeeAnn. It's like you have left me in the rearview mirror." This was a season in which I decided to look elsewhere to worship after nearly forty years in the same pew. I needed fresh perspective and to be outside my church and church culture checkbox for a season. Following God's lead, all I had to say prompted by Him was, "Yes, you're right."

What transpired was an hours-long conversation of my truthfulness. Transparency and humility, on both sides. Wise judgment and exacting discernment broke the twenty-year-old problem that could *never* have been fixed with Christian culture answers. It took God's outside-the-box solution and God's direct leading to answer both my husband's prayer and my dilemma. As Paul Tripp says in *New Morning Mercies*, "Truth isn't mean. Love isn't dishonest. They are two sides of the righteous agenda that longs for the spiritual welfare of another."[2]

The realtor I'd invited over to assess the value of our home (I was serious and driven) showed up completely confused to find two blithering crying souls. I turned her away. Right then, I used more sound judgment. I decided that instead of proceeding with divorce I would wait and flesh out what God might be doing with this radical and spiritual change in my husband. My obedience to God and my discerning judgment to find direction had led me here. Had I listened to Christian culture directives and dogma, I would *not* have arrived at this place of beautiful brokenness and my husband's heart change.

Though I do not know the future or how others' future choices will affect my life and decisions, I *do* know I will continue to seek and follow I AM every step of the way. I am going with God all the way, my true North!

Actual Wisdom and Sound Judgment

Sweet brothers and sisters, I hope you are pressing in to God for His truth, with your hearts tuned to His voice. I pray you use wise judgment as you paddle your river of life. Like in Assad's experience with Dave and the dream that came to him in jail, God's voice and path may not look as you expect. Like for me, both His answers and His direction may look *nothing* like you learned in Sunday school. Like nothing at all traditional.

Then again, what about God has *ever* been traditional? The description of our Savior in Revelation emits power and excitement to my broken and seeking spirit. Since the beginning of my journey in Chapter One, it has remained one of my favorite descriptions of God. Read it; marinate in it; meditate on it. Let this picture seep deep into your heart. Just *imagine I AM*!

> "After this I heard what sounded like the roar of a great multitude in heaven shouting:

> 'Hallelujah! Salvation and glory and power belong to our God, for true and just are his judgments.'"

> "I saw heaven standing open and there before me was a white horse, whose rider is called Faithful and True. With justice he judges and wages war. His eyes are like blazing fire, and on his head are many crowns. He has a name written on him that no one knows but he himself. He is dressed in a robe dipped in blood, and his name is the Word of God. The armies of heaven were following him, riding on white horses and dressed in fine linen, white and clean. Coming out of his mouth is a sharp sword with which to strike down the nations. He will rule them with an iron scepter. He treads the winepress of the fury of the wrath of God Almighty. On his robe and on his thigh he has this name written:

> KING OF KINGS AND LORD OF LORDS."
> (Revelation 19:1, 11–16)

Questions to Ponder:

1. What were your first impressions when reading through the section "The Ultimate Judge"? Describe the picture of God you saw when reading these verses. What feelings does that bring up in you?
2. Discuss an example of "friendly fire" in our current Christian culture.
3. Have you ever delivered or experienced a hammer in the hands of a "well-meaning" Christian about a personal experience like the ones mentioned? Share it while withholding names.
4. Share any experiences or thoughts about the honesty and humility required in recovery programs. Do you have anyone near you that is like a "BS" or "baloney meter"?
5. What are your experiences with "don't judge"? What do you think about our society's attitudes toward judging? Give some examples.
6. What thoughts in this chapter are new to you? How has this either changed or solidified your thinking about judging?
7. Take some time to think of people you have either harmed or dismissed by snap judgments. Confess them to the group if you feel comfortable. If realistic, make a plan to send a note or an email of apology.
8. Explain a splinter/log situation you've encountered. Be honest about your own judgments as well as the judgments of those who have launched into your story with chapter and verse.
9. Describe a new attribute of I AM He has shown you recently. How did you come to learn it and experience it?
10. Share a brief story about your "river of life" regarding sound judgment that was not the norm but that God directed. Who was on your rowing team?

CHAPTER ELEVEN

The Mish Mash Gospel Group or Real Body of Christ

*S*weet summertime! For many, the summer calendar permits more time for a good book, cookouts, beach lounging, mountain hikes, long vacations, or simple day trips to a local park. Summertime also brings changes to The Lamb Center. Similar to our national parks and museums, the number of visitors at The Lamb Center swells to record capacity. College students, youth groups, and families come in to help. Parents and youth pastors look for appropriate ways to get "tweens" and adolescents to engage with those who have less and to teach them to appreciate all they have and give back to society. These ideas are ingrained even in our secular world. Middle schools and high schools now include community service in their core curriculum. Mandatory volunteering sounds like an oxymoron to me, but exposure to the way other people live is a good outcome for sure.

On a hot Friday morning at The Lamb Center, I began the Bible study on a new book: Galatians. In doing so, I started with an explanation of the history and authorship of the book—not always exciting, but necessary to find similarities between that time period and our current world and make the study more relatable. Truly, Paul's strengthening of the church in Galatia against opinions of outsiders and ideologies of insiders is relevant in our society today. I decided to switch gears, though, when a group of eighth graders on a short mission trip joined us at the table. I shared the author Paul's conversion on the road to Damascus (Acts 9) and how his transformation filled him with passion to go on *his* many mission trips to let others know the truth of the gospel of Christ. In the Epistles, he warns each new church about distractions, false teaching, and meaningless philosophies. I explained how discernment and good judgment need good coaching, which the youth leaders seemed to appreciate. Then I challenged the guests, and particularly the young people, to check in with God and His word about *everything* they were taught by leaders. The kids seemed to love this. The lesson unfolded to include the truth that when anyone meets and follows Jesus, they change both direction and affections. Thank you, Holy Spirit, for guiding us as usual at The Lamb Center.

Good News

As we read the first chapter of Galatians, I noted the repetition of the word "gospel" and asked if anyone knew what that meant. No hands raised at first.

Finally, a homeless guest volunteered. "Good news." Bingo. Exact translation.

I prodded, "What *is* the good news?"

Reluctantly, a chaperone for one of the groups quietly said, "Jesus." Always a right and good answer at any Bible study. Bravo.

As the Holy Spirit would have it, we adjusted our lesson and reviewed the good news—the problem of sin and death (Romans 3:23; 6:23), the life-giving answer of the perfect sacrifice of Jesus on the cross for the forgiveness of our sins, and then His amazing resurrection so that we could live eternally with Him. It was a review of John 3:16. A guest volunteered to recite John 3:16 from memory in her broken English. Then a brave eighth-grade girl with sparkling eyes and braces shared a musical version of the verse that she had learned in grade school from a nun. It was a lovely lesson highlighted by the stories of the guests and visitors about life transformation. The guests ended up preaching to the students through their testimonies. The impact was palpable. It was the basics of our shared faith in Jesus and the eternal life we share when we receive the good news of the gospel. Even though as many denominations, ideas, passions, opinions, and circumstances surrounded the table as there were people, the glue was Jesus, the Christ. That is the *real* Church, the body of Christ.

I was reminded of the harmonizing quote, "In essentials unity, in nonessentials liberty, and in all things charity." This quote, often attributed to Augustine, was actually found in a 1627 tract during a particularly bloody time in Christian history, the Thirty Years' War.[1] The world needs this sentiment now more than ever. The essentials of our faith, the gospel, need to be articulated well as our world looks for answers.

The fresh Breath of life in me, guidance from the Holy Spirit, aided me in spotting the truth of the gospel through ordinary, broken people and their stories. I did not put a lid on what He was doing. Where the Spirit of God is, there is freedom (2 Corinthians 3:17). It was different from the church culture in which I grew up. I witnessed firsthand the power of God to do His will through the gifts He gave to His people. By allowing the Holy Spirit to work through whomever He wants, however He wants, for God's purpose and His glory, we witness the amazing work of God and get to participate with Him. Isn't this what believers should be doing and experiencing?

This eclectic group and serendipitous study caused me to think about church culture and what wasn't working. A thirst for God's abundant real life, not just for me but for the body of Christ, had been stirring up in me for quite some time.

Thirsty

Maybe you feel a stirring too. Most Christians I know are thirsty for wholehearted living, real answers to real problems, and authentic relationships as they follow Jesus in this complicated life. We want to be in community with fellow believers as we fulfill our purpose and destiny with God. In the book of Acts, we get a sense that believers experienced camaraderie with fellow believers during a difficult time for the new church. Persecution produced communion. Difficulty encouraged sharing the load and helping brothers and sisters along. In our difficult postmodern world with shrinking moral absolutes and near hostility toward the gospel, the thirst of our soul is for much of the same. We need real community, compassion, and authenticity now more than ever.

Surely some find balm for their deep and real aches within the institutional church. Some churches run programs like Celebrate Recovery, have places for AA meetings, have authentic small groups, and address difficult topics like pornography and teen suicide. They might even hold on to sound biblical doctrine while dealing with the reality of this complicated life. Sadly, though, those churches with both are the exceptions.

Many stick with church but find community in Bible studies outside the church or secular recovery groups. Many have jumped ship from church buildings altogether. Josh Packard, in his book *Church Refugees*,[2] gives us statistics for the growing trend. There are sixty million plus who are "done" and about thirty million who are "almost done" with the institutional church. But they both serve God and follow Him passionately in other environments. "Dones," as Packard refers to them, were very active in their churches but report having increased trouble with the "structure, message, and politics of the institutional church." They aren't permitted to use their gifts fully and are not experiencing authentic community. Dones don't leave the institutional church after just one bad experience. They "often work(ed) for years to reform the church from within."[3] Perhaps most importantly, Dones don't necessarily leave with bitterness; they leave with sadness. Truly, the Dones haven't left the Church. They, along with the believers who still attend, *are* the Church, the body of Christ. We are one (Romans 12:5).

Tragically, many others leave the institutional church and no longer associate with any designation of faith. They believe

God is just within those institutional church walls and perceive they don't fit the mold at all. Because of the lack of community or because they don't agree with what is said from the pulpit, tired of hypocrisy, they leave the church and stop following God altogether. They may have committed their lives to Jesus ages ago, but they listen to the outside culture's wisdom because Christian culture's wisdom seems so out of kilter. They drift away from the faith altogether.

In addition, Dr. James Emery White describes another alarming trend in his 2015 book, *The Continued Rise of the Nones*. The "nones," a growing statistic (twenty percent of Americans), are those who have no designation in regard to faith. In the millennial age group, the percentage is a whopping thirty-three percent and growing.[4]

Regardless of designation, many of us who are involved in the traditional churches of our day have a dull but knowing feeling something is missing. Something in our lives fell apart, and the church programs don't fit the need. The lack of authentic community gives us no room to bring our angst, pain, real-life drama, or even our volunteer efforts back into the fellowship of believers. God is still establishing His kingdom. So we must follow His lead in these latter days.

Inspired by the positive experiences each week at The Lamb Center Bible study, I decided to inspect the history of my relationship with the church.

Introspection

In various seasons of life, I have enjoyed popular inductive Bible studies. These nondenominational groups promote peaceful community in the study of the written Word of God. At different times over the course of twenty-five years, I was part of the leadership team for them. Through that training, I learned to study the Bible in depth and practice the "tolerance" of different doctrine within the community of faith in Christ. I learned to respect others' opinions while peacefully expressing mine.

Men and women from a wide variety of denominations study alongside simple seekers with no church affiliation. There are rules in place to keep specific churches, preachers, politics, and the like out of the discussion, so as not to cause division. We weren't to discuss commentaries, popular books, or blogs either. The individual, the indwelling Holy Spirit, and the written Word of God were shared in community. Church community in authenticity. It is simple, yet profound. The ladies in my small groups, year after year, became my *real* body of Christ for most of my adult life.

I did notice, however, that those outside the Bible-believing community were talked about with a bit of disdain, with "us" and "them" lingo which kept my mind and heart from listening well to those outside the community of faith. Instead, I listened only to jump in with the exact chapter and verse of the right answer, which is never ideal for wooing someone to faith in the gospel.

It's Complicated

My church experience was more complex. Having been in the same church since age three, it has been a place of identity, not necessarily community. Although I had brief seasons of exploring other local churches, I was nearly shamed back by close family members. It's where I *belong,* right?

In my church, probably like yours, we believe and recite the same doctrine and creeds. One isn't invited into conversation about differences of opinions but rather must get on board with what the denomination asserts. Or else leave. Or start a revolt. Sadly, this happens in many churches, and over issues as small as the placement of a drum set on the altar. Gasp! So, like with many churches, at mine, many people have come and gone. We rarely know where they went or why.

Sundays when the "Friendship Register" gets passed back and forth down the pew, I long for an additional designation. Besides "regular attender," "member," "guest/first time visitor," and "requesting a call," there should a place for "It's complicated!" It *is* good to be known, even in a large church, especially in an area like ours. However, I struggle with my identity in this church membership I have had for so long. If statistics prove right, you too have a multifaceted relationship with designating your church attendance and involvement. It *is* complicated; we can't fit our entire experience into a little checkbox.

I did *try* to make my church a real place of community. I served in various places over the decades. Oddly, it was my entrance into social media that gave me a better opportunity to know other members beyond their facades. I knew when they had trials, new babies, exciting vacations, or specific needs. It made the experience on Sundays more connected, with real questions and content to discuss instead of meaningless how-do-you-dos.

Years ago, I joined a small group from my church to engage in community. I wanted to be known as an adult with my own identity (instead of family of origin and marriage connections) and connect with this body of Christ I'd known since toddler years. At one meeting, though, I got into a rather heated discussion with a strict Calvinist and found myself uninvited from further meetings. Case in point. He was the leader, and I wasn't on board. The reputation of excellence in teaching and formatted worship services that my church had and valued left little room for my talents and wisdom.

But again, I tried. My proposal to teach a women's Bible study (about exploring deep heart matters) alongside my friend was greeted with initial excitement, but from there came red tape that got more and more tangled as we progressed. At first, we suggested an already written and popular study as the curriculum, but it was rejected for its differing denominational perspective; so my friend and I (both long-time members of the church and students of the Bible) ended up writing our own plan and study. Still, all had to be approved by the newly hired young women's director. Our writing was henpecked and edited to a barely recognizable version of the original, and we were relegated to the basement choir room, with one of our breakout sessions in the men's choir robe room (I kid you not). The bulletin announced it as the "Women's Bible Study with [director's name] and various teachers." My girlfriend and I had some good laughs. For years afterward, we referred to each other as "various teacher." The small group of women who attended were blessed, but the effort was just a sample of my salmon swimming upstream experience. That was the end of my efforts to serve at my own church of nearly fifty years. My church didn't seem to need my real-life answers or efforts. I stayed in my pew as an observer and began to serve God elsewhere.

A first step was running an Alpha group (a program that explains Christianity to those who would like to know but aren't so fond of going to institutional churches)[5] in my home for neighbors. It was sponsored by my church, so an elder had to oversee my steps. The elder asked to schedule his visit for the session about the Holy Spirit so he could explain our church's views, as they differed slightly from the recorded session. Seriously? I went rogue, played the tape, and taught the session myself. I let the participants discern for themselves what they should believe with all the evidence laid out.

Meanwhile, a more liberal church in the neighborhood welcomed me with open arms. I wrote another curriculum for their week-long class for little ones on worship (which I didn't even think to offer my own church after the aforementioned experiences). I was given swift pause when the pastor (I had respectfully submitted my notes and outline because you are supposed to submit all outgoing information to the leader, right?) loved it but recommended I use more gender-neutral terms for God so as not to confuse the children. I swiftly answered that email with "If Jesus calls God 'Father,' so will I." She graciously welcomed my teaching and views. Open-minded is open-minded.

Paradoxical Pride of Belonging

Although it is grounding to be on the same page of beliefs with my church, it caused me to develop arrogance toward outsiders, even other believers. The theologically sound teaching from our church had all the "right" answers to the world's problems, and I would conjure them whenever I encountered someone with a different perspective. Whenever I "enlightened" someone else in Bible studies outside my church, there was a tinge of pride in my response. *We* were right. I kindly tolerated differing opinions but didn't let theirs into my heart or mind. *I* knew better. My pride was off-putting. I wasn't drawing others into community, nor was I fostering conversation. I was shutting people down with my know-it-all persona. Maya Angelou said it most beautifully: "I've learned that people will forget what you said, people will forget what you did, but people will never forget how you made them feel." I think it is the same way with truth. A lot depends on delivery. Jesus knew that extraordinarily well.

Many of these experiences I have mentioned may be similar to yours. They leave us whiplashed, going from being the wounded to wounding others. These extremes may leave a new believer perplexed and the world at large questioning our unity of faith. It is similar to the early apostles and the church of Galatia, who faced both self-righteous "Judaizers" (those who put additional, unnecessary burdens of faith back in place) and heretical false teachers who wormed their way into the church.

Like Paul, we recognize *all* churches are flawed because they are filled and led by depraved human beings (Romans 3:9-19)! Each epistle is a Wisdom 101 class of either encouragement or a faith-filled smackdown, depending on what each church needed. Though, we, like Jesus, love His Church (an assembly of Christians) for which He died (Acts 20:28).

As you read these descriptions about extremes, try to relax. Instead of finger-pointing, begin an introspection of your own. Wisdom, discernment, and sound judgment lie somewhere in between. If you are reading this book, you are not likely in either of the extremes. But if the Spirit convicts, well, that's His work!

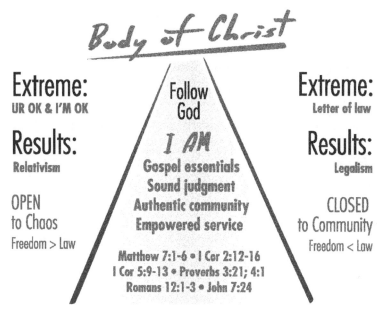

Figure #3

Loosey Goosey

The first extreme in Figure #3 is epitomized by the 1970s mantra of "I'm OK, you're OK." Everything, every choice, is heroic and brave. This extreme is the most likely place in which people feel welcomed into the faith. Among those who struggle with the confusion of trauma, sin, or poor teaching, the lack of concern for right and wrong—the slippery slope of indulgence—replaces the practice of penance. There is no guilt because there are no sins, except calling something a sin. This extreme makes Jesus' sacrifice meaningless. This Jesus spins in a field, accepting anything and anyone just as they are. Gandhi may just as well replace Jesus, because there is nothing that makes His life or death significant. Sin and forgiveness have no meaning. Whenever you have no boundaries and no rules, you leave yourself open to chaos. Here tolerance is deemed better than wisdom. The only sin is judgment. Relativism marks the spot on this extreme in the faith.

Recently, I ran into a woman who had a beautiful umbrella that looked like a rainbow. I laughed at the irony and said, "Now *that* is clever." When she looked confused, I said, "You know, no epic floods?" Apparently the sentiment was lost on her amid the August downpour. Of course, the rainbow's original meaning is not actually diversity but God's own symbol of His promise that He will never again grow so fed up with us that He will flood the world (Genesis 9:9–15). Though the symbol of rainbow flags of diversity is often used by this extreme, they are absolutely right about one thing. God is *indeed* still speaking.

The Righteous Rigid

The other extreme seems to pick a few sins that seem the worst of all. Years ago, and to some extent today, harsh judgment was shown to those with shattered marriages. It seemed the cardinal sin of divorce was the line in the sand separating the good from the bad. No one bothered to investigate just how "good" those other marriages were. Staying together, regardless of the health of the marriage, was deemed the pinnacle of goodness and godliness. A divorcee, even one who had been cheated on, was forbidden to teach Sunday school or be in leadership of any kind. Some were even banished from membership. More recently it seems abortion, homosexuality, and various sexual preferences are deemed the worst sins of all.

Truly, God has plenty to say about *all* sin, for which Jesus died. Indeed, His standards have not changed (Numbers 23:19). He doesn't talk about them on the sliding scale of relativism like the first extreme. But this extreme of the faith speaks about certain sins with an air of pride as it smugly points fingers. The truth is Jesus has more to say about pride than many of the other sins. Though Jesus died for all sins, those with a plank in their eye find it hard to see what is really happening with other hurting and sinful human beings (Matthew 7:3–5).

Ironically, many other sins committed *against* the folks struggling with the sins I mentioned are egregious. Why aren't these same churches speaking out about the date rape that might have occurred before an abortion, or the sexual abuse from a priest that potentially led a young boy to question his sexuality, or the verbal abuse that perhaps led a woman to get a divorce? This is just a sampling of judgment from one extreme of our Christian faith.

This extreme keeps people closed off from authentic community. Our sins become secrets that cannot be shared or processed, creating a mask of pride. And with that mask in place, believers in this extreme seem to follow the letter of the law, resulting in a rigid and legalistic approach to life. Casualties include those shamed away from Jesus, likely leaving the faith altogether or running into the open arms of the other extreme.

In the Zone

Between these extremes, not lukewarm (Revelation 3:16), is *exactly* where we need to be. Shown in Figure #3, the "middle" is where the individual believer (a living stone and temple of God) finds the body of Christ (an assembly of stones and temples). Together people worship and serve the unchanging *and* loving God, I AM. *This* body of Christ is a *community* that both promotes and assists its own with sound judgment on the path of life across this world's rocky terrain. This community of faith has safe boundaries, respectful relationships, empowered service, and the gospel as its sure foundation. Here believers with the mind of Christ (1 Corinthians 2:16) mature in both their knowledge of God and His Word. *And* they serve God with their gifting as they wisely listen to Him.

Transitional Transformation

Although I continue to worship at my home church most Sundays, I am in a new place of understanding God, having been exposed to a variety of backgrounds of the Christian faith at The Lamb Center. Additionally, my participation in prayer at a group called *Rescued for Destiny* has really rocked my world. Although most attendees are "Dones" (not attending institutional churches but following God passionately), they seem more in tune with Him daily, moment by moment, than many faithful churchgoers. We listen to the still-speaking God as we pray. At The Lamb Center, with the essentials of the good news firmly in place, I have the liberty to teach and lead the Bible study as the Holy Spirit leads. Many of the staff and volunteers are clergy from a variety of denominations, with various seminary degrees, and they participate in my lessons at the Bible study as fellow believers, not as superiors. Not only am I known among them, but I am known for my identity in Christ, respected for my wisdom and perspective. It is DeeAnn (a new creation in Christ) plus God, I AM (the author and finisher of my faith), doing what only God plus me can do together. In that role I feel the freedom God intended for His children.

Because the outside veneer of church world is off display and the pride is stripped away, we can better imagine what I AM had in mind for the kingdom of God.

The "shoulds" and the flow charts of hierarchy and appearances are also stripped away. The Holy Spirit is large and in charge. I've found that His presence and grace make all the difference when it comes to heart change and transformation.

It is as St. Maria of Paris said: "Christ, who approached prostitutes, tax collectors and sinners, can hardly be the teacher of those who are afraid to soil their pristine garments, who are completely devoted to the letter, who live only by the rules, and who govern their whole life according to rules."

KISS - Keep It Simple, ~~Stupid~~ Sweetie

Having seen Jesus successfully answer the complicated trick questions of the Sadducees, the Pharisees, experts in the Law, decided to take a crack at Him. "Teacher, which is the most important commandment in the law of Moses?" they asked him (Matthew 22:36 NLT). Jesus made very plain the heart of the matter: "You must love the Lord your God with all your heart, all your soul, and all your mind. This is the first and greatest commandment. A second is equally important: 'Love your neighbor as yourself.' The entire law and all the

demands of the prophets are based on these two command-
ments" (Matthew 22:37–40 NLT). He took the whole Old and
New Testament and boiled it down. Boom. We complicate
things. As my sweet cousin Jay says, "Love God; love people.
It's just that simple."

Foundations for Living

In 1 Corinthians 2, Paul, orator extraordinaire, makes it
plain. He preaches only Christ crucified, his redemptive, sub-
stitutionary death and resurrection—the good news—"so that
your faith would not rest on the wisdom *and* rhetoric of men,
but on the Power of God" (1 Corinthians 2:5 AMP). He goes
on to plead for unity in judgment about the gospel (essentials of
the faith) and then affirms that as we mature in Christ, we can
know the secrets God Himself reveals to us through His Spirit.
And amazingly, we develop the "mind of Christ." We can use
wise judgment because God reveals these things to you and to
me, fellow dwellings of the Holy Spirit!

"Do you not know *and* understand that you [the church] are
the temple of God, and that the Spirit of God dwells [perma-
nently] in you [collectively and individually]?" (1 Corinthians
3:16 AMP). Both individually and collectively, the Spirit of
God dwells in us! It's like micro—we are a temple—and
macro—we are *in* the community of the body of Christ, which
is also a temple.

"You also, like living stones, are being built into a spiritual
house to be a holy priesthood" (1 Peter 2:5). We are the "bride
of Christ" making ourselves ready and awaiting His return
(Revelation 19:7).

Imagine the amazing things that will happen as each of
us, without hindrance from leaders, seeks, hears, and does
what God says. God, who is in charge of all, participates with
believers in building the body of Christ in maturity to attain the
whole measure of the fullness of Christ (Ephesians 4:11–12).

> The Lord is at the head of the column. He leads
> them with a shout! (Joel 2:11 NLT)

In an article by Lonnie Lane, in a blog called *Messianic Vision*, we learn that although the Greek word *ecclesia* is translated *church* in the New Testament, it isn't an accurate picture of how we envision church today. A more precise translation of *ecclesia* is "body." William Tyndale, in the sixteenth century, felt that *church* didn't cut it either and changed it to *congregation*. "They obviously meant a body of Believers in Messiah Yeshua summoned by God and called out (by Him) from among the Jewish and Roman peoples to come together into a separate community under His Lordship."[6]

In Acts 17:1–6, we read of Paul and Silas being accused of turning the world (system) upside down. Ms. Lane comically asserts that Paul and Silas weren't "church builders" in the sense that we may think. "They weren't advocating people now find some place where they can be separate and not influence anyone around them, meeting for a few hours on the weekend and singing a few songs, hearing a message and then going home! These men were Kingdom builders!"[7] They were building with *living stones*!

Furthermore, Rick Joyner, in *Visions of the Harvest*, asserts that while it was said of the early believers, "They turned the world upside down," it will be said of those following hard after God in these latter days, "*They* have turned an upside-down world right-side up."[8] May we *be* those living stones as we humbly follow God to build and strengthen His kingdom.

The Lamb Center Mish Mash

Acts 17:24 says, "God, who made the world and everything in it, since He is Lord of heaven and earth, does not dwell in temples made with hands" (AMP). However, we need to continue to meet together to encourage each other in the faith as we await Jesus' return (Hebrews 10:25). Believer, use sound judgment with your mind of Christ to find a community of believers, fellow temples, whether it's inside or outside the institutional church.

In the mishmash of broken stories, mine included, that come around the table at The Lamb Center, I see the radiance of Jesus. I feel the delight of the Holy Spirit. I sense the love of our Father as we, volunteers and guests, alike listen to each other, honor each other, and walk in our gifting, holding fast to God's holy Word. We encourage, challenge, worship, and exhort. Though a mismatched group of "wretched," "miserable," "poor," "blind," and "naked" people, we are fellow image bearers of the King of kings! We are family, His body in community.

> Hear the call of the kingdom
> Lift your eyes to the King
> Let His song rise within you
> As a fragrant offering
> Of how God rich in mercy
> Came in Christ to redeem
> All who trust in His unfailing grace
>
> Hear the call of the Kingdom
> To be children of light
> With the mercy of heaven
> The humility of Christ
> Walking justly before Him
> Loving all that is right
> That the life of Christ may shine through us
>
> Hear the call of the Kingdom
> To reach out to the lost
>
> With the Father's compassion
> In the wonder of the cross
> Bringing peace and forgiveness
> And a hope yet to come
> Let the nations put their trust in Him

King of Heaven we will answer the call
We will follow bringing hope to the world
Filled with passion, filled with power to proclaim
Salvation in Jesus' name

—*Hear the Call of the Kingdom* by Keith & Kristyn Getty

Questions to Ponder:

Before the discussion, please read aloud together:
"In essentials unity, in nonessentials liberty, and in all things charity."

As always, please be respectful to withhold names and specific churches. Having just read the judging chapter, we understand how snap judgments with all-knowing pride can wound. Pause before you answer every question . . . except the first one!

1. What would your perfect summertime day look like?
2. How do you explain the gospel, the "good news"?
3. When and where did you last experience the freedom of Christ in the body of Christ?
4. Why do you think the Dones are on the rise? Are you a Done, or do you know any?
5. Why do you think the Nones are on the rise? Are you a None, or do you know any?
6. If a church membership status of "it's complicated" resonates with you, share your situation.
7. If you have found it, explain your "zone."

CHAPTER TWELVE

Joy to the World or <u>*Rescued for Destiny*</u>

"Kyrie Eleison!" ("Lord, have mercy!") a woman with a tormented daughter cries out to Jesus (Matthew 15:22).

"Kyrie Eleison!" two blind men call out to Him, asking for the help only He can give (Matthew 20:30–31).

I can relate. I bet you can too.
"Kyrie Eleison!" Life can be hard. Yet God tells us He has a good plan and we get to participate. Filled with successes, disappointments, hopes, heartbreaks, dreams, *and* possibilities, life often can feel like a wild roller coaster, or to some more like the carnival game of Whac-A-Mole!

Consequently, and tragically, many Christians disengage from the vibrancy of life and live day-to-day lives in the doldrums of "meh." Many live with regret, sure they have missed the original design—the promise of a purposeful life. And many lower expectations and settle for the manicured lawn illusions of "suburbia," whether they live in the suburbs or not. Yet, I agree with Howard Macy: "The spiritual life cannot be made suburban. It is always a frontier and we who live in it must accept and even rejoice that it remains untamed."[1]

In *The Sacred Romance*, John Eldredge articulates the reality well: "We have been rescued, but still the choice is ours to stay in our small stories, clutching our household gods and false lovers, or run in search of life."[2] I add, *abundant* life!

Names and Faces

Working the front desk at The Lamb Center, I get to know many names and faces. However, because I'm there only two days a week, I don't always get to know the origin, progress, or process of all the guests' stories. Much like our church homes, people come and go, and we don't always know why.

It can be dangerous living on the streets and in the woods. Outcomes can be cruel. Bad news spreads and disheartens like wildfire. Incarceration. Hospitalization. Overdose. Death. One dear guest adventured to Florida. Upon departure, he cheerfully asked folks to keep in touch through his PO Box in the warmer climate. Months later, we learned he had been in a terrible motorcycle accident and lost his life. For obvious reasons like these, there is always nervous apprehension when I ask a staff member, "What ever happened to . . . ?"

On the flip side, there is the good news. It encourages others, although it spreads at a slower, but steady, rate. One former guest comes back regularly as a volunteer on her days off from work. She has housing and a steady job. She joyfully prays, "Lord, I praise and thank You for another day and all You have done to save me," when asked to pray in the circle before a meal or Bible study. Another guest won the coveted Employee of the Month award at his job and brought the plaque back to Dave to hang in his office, as he did not have a wall to hang it on yet. Another teaches a regular Bible study at The Lamb Center, and yet another is a manager at a large retail store, where his kind treatment of the employees inspires loyalty and great service. My guess is many who move on from The Lamb Center with the hope of a brilliant future don't always come back to let others know. A reminder of hardship may be the last place on earth someone would want to revisit. Perfectly under-standable. But it is a treat when they do.

Cast of Contributors

Another way I see people coming and going through The Lamb Center front door is through donations. People come at all hours with all kinds of donations of food, clothing, and toiletries. It's one of the perks of working the front desk—I can see what folks bring. I can cheerfully say, "God bless you" and mean it. In such a position, you get an idea of the span of the body of Christ and its gifts. You see what creative acts of service and giving can mean to the guests who have nothing. Homemade knit hats made by an elderly woman in winter. Hard-boiled eggs delivered daily by another dear family. Hotel toiletries from a business woman who travels weekly across the country for meetings. A new volunteer came to us during a brief break in her upward corporate ladder climb. She told me, "Honestly, I know my gift of making money in my field is my best gift to this special place. I can't wait to send my donations back to The Lamb Center after seeing firsthand how it works!"

One Monday, a distinguished gentleman walked in, clearly in a hurry for work in his suit and tie. He handed me an envelope.

"Do you want a receipt, sir?" I asked.

"No, thank you," he said as he rushed back out the door before I could say, "God bless you."

Patti was nearby. We always give cash and checks directly to staff as soon as possible. Those donations keep our doors open; they are valuable and urgent. When I handed the enve-lope to her, she had already watched the man come and go. Her eyes brimmed with tears. Perplexed, thinking we might be in the midst of particularly hard times, I begged for an answer.

"He used to be a guest years ago. *What* a miracle!"

Not Just a Job, an Adventure

One of my newer rituals when things are quiet at the entrance (which is rare) is to go through all the mail in the slots from A to Z to see if there are any pieces that have accumulated or perhaps could be distributed to a guest who is present.

One Monday, when I had reached the Ls, I came across a stack of mail for Paul L. Hmm. I hadn't seen him in quite some time. I wondered what had happened to him. Because I was particularly fond of this young man, I flagged down Patti to ask. She cheerfully responded, "He got a job!" Praise God! This is the outcome we always pray for, but because many of the jobs out there are basic hourly jobs, far beneath the expectations of some of our guests, it doesn't always last. Recovering from the nosedive of possible addiction or incarceration takes time, diligence, and motivation. It is particularly difficult to stay driven when you have no consistent place to lay your head at night.

It wasn't a few hours later when Paul bounced in happily with a bag of laundry to be processed. He looked glowingly well. Serendipitous providence! I gave him his bundle of mail and asked how he was doing. "Great!" he exclaimed. His job as a tour guide in a downtown DC museum was the perfect fit. He was beaming as he explained the thorough training he'd been through and all the fascinating facts he'd learned and memorized. His passion for history and his mind for details combined with his enthusiasm and extroverted personality lined up with the need for guides during the peak of tourist season. He said, "You won't *believe* it. People hand me twenty-dollar bills as *tips*! I leave at the end of the day with fistfuls of money, and that isn't even the best part of the job. I have fun. I love my job!" My heart swelled with his.

Finding Your Groove

One of my favorite things in all the earth is seeing someone find their groove. Find their passion. Find their "sweet spot" in life. I've witnessed it in the sparkling eyes of a roller skating waitress whistling as she balanced stacks of plates in Marina Del Rey. I've seen it deep under the earth in Luray Caverns, in a guide who practically salivated while describing stalactites. I've observed it in the grateful words of a farmer delighting in the miracle of working the land to produce fruit. I've heard it in the voice of a college student glistening with delight while explaining algorithms to a younger student. I've even heard it in a small but strong lawyer saying, "I *live* for justice. I don't know what it is within me, but every fiber of my being joins together to defend the weak and vulnerable from tyrants." And I've heard it in Paul from The Lamb Center, describing how he exuberantly shares his new knowledge with interested tourists. Wow. I hear it right now through my open window as a man whistles while he works, joyfully landscaping my neighbor's yard. These folks have found purpose and delight in their jobs or careers. But I think God is about more.

The word *vocation* has more to do with a spiritual calling in life, and it may have very little to do with a job. In fact, the Latin word *vocare* means "to call." Frederick Buechner, in *Wishful Thinking: A Seeker's ABC*, defines it beautifully: "The place God calls you to is the place where your deep gladness and the world's deep hunger meet."[3] So truly we can find our vocation in raising our kids, rescuing pets, writing curriculum, feeding the homeless, prayer-walking through our neighborhood, being an active voice in our community, writing op-eds in the newspaper, playing gospel music at festivals, or testifying before congressional hearings on human rights. These may have nothing to do with a job *or* a career; this is *vocation*. That sounds invitingly better and encompasses more of real life.

Greedy

I don't know about you, but I want *even* more! I want to fulfill my God-given destiny. All of it. Destiny and desire, only a few letters apart, are intrinsically linked. Sadly, neither are mentioned much in Christian circles. We seem to be rather okay doing church once a week and going to our nine-to-five jobs, an endless hamster wheel, to get by. When did our poetic souls die? When did, "Watch over your heart with all diligence, for from it *flow* the springs of life" (Proverbs 4:23 AMP) go away? John Eldredge states in his book *Journey of Desire*, "Christianity is not an invitation to become a moral person. It is not a program for getting us in line or for reforming society. At its core, Christianity begins with an invitation to desire."[4]

In exploring the faith, some may say, "Follow your heart." Others say, "Kill desire, lest sin crop up." Yet, once we receive Christ into our hearts, although we still struggle with sin, we have a soft and beautiful heart, one after His (Ezekiel 36:26). Our hearts and desires aren't bad. They were put there by our Maker. He has made us a new creation (2 Corinthians 5:17).

Jesus Himself said, "I have come that they may have life and have it to the full" (John 10:10). David G. Benner, in his deep and soul-searching book *Desiring God's Will* says, "God invites us to share the animating and generative life that is our origin and destiny."[5]

The Magnificent Designer

I AM. Where we began. And in Whom we began. In a sermon about Jeremiah, Rector David Hanke of Restoration Anglican Church in Arlington, Virginia, expresses the amazing reality about each of us. Before you had a body, God already knew and delighted in your soul. He had plans for every day of your life before you even came to be (Psalm 139). Mind-blowing.

I love *The Message's* paraphrase of Romans 11:36: "Have you ever come on anything quite like this extravagant generosity of God, this deep, deep wisdom? It's way over our heads. We'll never figure it out. Is there anyone around who can explain God? Anyone smart enough to tell him what to do? Anyone who has done him such a huge favor that God has to ask his advice? Everything comes from him; Everything happens through him; Everything ends up in him. Always glory! Always praise! Yes. Yes. Yes."

He who calls you into your destiny also knows all things. God has many-sided wisdom in infinite variety and innumerable aspects, and through Jesus we have free access, an unreserved approach, to God (Ephesians 3:10–12 AMP). He has plans and purposes that are beyond even our hearts and desires. He can do exceedingly, abundantly more than we ask, hope, or think (Ephesians 3:20). So putting all our eggs in His basket is wise! All things are held together by I AM (Colossians 1:17). He has the expert advantage to see inside, through, and forward to walk us into the destiny in our future, after the destiny of each day has elapsed.

Our Magnificent Participation

We limit our amazing God. And. We limit our amazing souls He designed for greatness. We need to participate. In the parable of the talents (Matthew 25:14–30), we learn that God gives us different gifts and treasures. He expects us to use them and develop them for His glory. Not only do we need to participate, but we *get* to participate as well! We get a choice to join God in His plans for us. And with that, we must choose to learn the skills of following God into our destiny He designed. They include listening. They include seeing. They include desire. They include passion. And most of all, they *require* cooperation with His Spirit intertwined with ours.

Imagine! Participating with the God of the universe in His plans and purposes for us and the world. It doesn't get any better than that. Sherry Colley of Rescued for Destiny says, "Destiny is so much bigger than purpose. Destiny encompasses all the purposes and all the plans that All of God has for All of You. What's best is that you get to do them together with Him, as well as with others!"[6]

How do you become all of you and come to know all of God? You do what we've been talking about all along. You go to I AM and strip Christian image, what you think you're supposed to be and who you think God is. Ask I AM to reveal Himself to you and to reveal and remove any "Christian culture" in your thinking. Tell Him you want to go to the depths of your heart. Ask Him where He wants to start and go with Him there. You can get a good idea of it by looking around you and seeing what the obstacles and roadblocks in your life have been so far.

The more you know Him, what He gives you dominion and authority over, and the places deep in your heart, the more you can begin to do and execute all I AM designed for you to be and do. Daniel 11:32 says, "The people who know their God shall prove themselves strong *and* shall stand firm and do exploits [for God]" (AMP). Day by day. Moment by moment. You participate with Him. A you-plus-God, one-in-a-jillion destiny. To get a glimpse of what your destiny might look like, look only to God and to what sets your heart ablaze. When His Spirit is planted in your heart, your spirit and His are molded together. They become intrinsically connected. You press on to take hold of that for which Christ Jesus took hold of you (Philippians 3:12–14). He becomes the prize (Genesis 15:1), and He is *calling* you.

It's Easy to Miss

We need to stay in step with the Holy Spirit and God's leading (Galatians 5:25). In these latter days, those between the cross and Jesus' return, we know from Acts 2:17 that men and women *will* see visions and dream dreams. Older folks will have dreams of significance. We are told continually to stay alert for those times. No one is exempt. All the while, we are to be about God's business and the things He has assigned us to do (Ephesians 2:10). It doesn't take a pair of glasses to see that our world and many of the lives around us are imploding. There is much that I AM plus you need to do. Be alert!

In Samuel's day, dreams and visions were rare (1 Samuel 3:1). So when the direct call of God comes to Samuel, he almost misses it. Although a child in the temple, he hears the voice of God (literally) calling out to him and three times mistakes it for Eli, the high priest. Finally, Eli realizes it's the LORD who is calling Samuel and instructs him to respond, "Speak, Lord, for your servant is listening" (1 Samuel 3:10 AMP). Samuel then responds to the One who is actually calling him. And God speaks to him about many important things.

This is the first time Samuel hears directly from God, but not the last. Throughout Samuel's life, he faithfully delivers all-important messages from God to His people and does all

God gives him to do, like anoint David as king, who was the true heart ancestor of Jesus Christ.

Without the proper response to the One who was calling, Samuel could have missed his destiny. Believer, it is *scary* he almost missed it! This biblical figure, in a temple, almost missed it. We have so many more distractions. His cry of "Speak, Lord, for your servant is listening" is the same cry we must utter directly to God. Not to the pastor, not to another person, but to the One who calls us.

Are you listening?! Be sure to pay attention and respond. Day by day. Seek. Listen. Obey. Go to the heart of the matter. Pursue all of God and all of who you are in Him. *This* is the stuff of destiny!

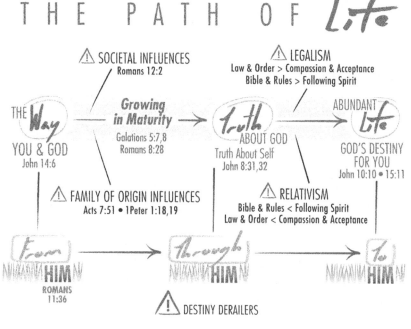

Figure #4

We're all on a path, or river, or adventure of life (Figure #4). We begin our new life, or "way," when we accept Jesus. As we mature in the faith, we learn more truth about God and more truth about ourselves. Many distractions attempt to derail us along the journey into our destiny toward abundant life, as we have discussed in previous chapters. I call them "destiny derailers." *But God.* Again, that wonderful transition. "We are assured *and* know that [God being a partner in their labor] all things work together *and* are [fitting into a plan] for good to *and* for those who love God and are called according to [His] design *and* purpose." (Romans 8:28 AMP). We can see that, indeed, all things are "from Him, and through Him, and to Him" (Romans 11:36 AMP).

Jesus, as our human example, gives us a pattern, a path to follow; He shows us how to live deeply *true* lives in Him. We can fulfill our destinies in, through, and for God. *Real* life to the full.

Do You Want to Know Something Amazing About Me?

"Do you want to know something amazing about me?" Of all the darling things I've heard kids say, this is one of my favorites. I was just being introduced to this precocious five-year-old when she blurted it out, as if impatient with the tiresome pleasantries. Truly, let's get to the *real* stuff.

To her question, I answered with a big "Yes!"

She responded, "Everyone at school wants to be around me because I am such a great leader."

Ah, that we were all so positive about all that is amazing about us and what God is doing in us and through us.

So. Do you want to know something amazing about *me*?! Well, now that I'm a heck of a lot more real than I used to be, I'll tell you.

As I have pressed in to God for more of the real Him and more of the real me, I have become an extremely well person. More like the original design God created me to be. I feel it from my head to my toes. Am I perfect? Heavens, not even close. Ask anyone who knows me! Have I become more wholly me? Yes. Have I learned more about I AM? Yes. Do I feel more connected and confident with what He has me do, pray, say, and express on a daily basis? Yes. Have I recognized in the moment what is *not* okay, what is fake, and isn't of God? Yes. Am I quick to ask God what is cropping up in me? If it is about my sin or a stuck part of me that needs to be rescued? Yes. Do I notice what needs to be addressed and what can just be dropped off my radar for another person to handle? You bet. Have I begun to walk into my destiny? YES. *This* is what it looks like.

This is a day-by-day unfolding of my destiny, a magnificent part of the whole. My part in the kingdom of God. My part in the royal priesthood and holy nation God desires and deserves (1 Peter 2:9; Exodus 19:6; Revelation 5:10). I am part of the bride of Christ, making herself ready (Revelation 19:7).

Like Paul, I have found a "sweet spot" in life. I feel like I am doing something that blends with my gifts and calling. Teaching at The Lamb Center. Writing this book. Speaking at conferences and retreats. But, like Paul experienced as well, there are disappointments in life even a groove can't lift. It isn't always sunshine and smiles in the path of life, even when you are doing what you feel called to do.

It might come as a surprise to you that during the writing of this chapter I have experienced some really tough family struggles. Really bad things have happened. Circumstances I did not choose are in my path. But oddly, I find myself confidently smiling with God. We are in sync. I look at these obstacles, and instead of feeling exasperated (although sometimes I do get worn-down physically and take needed rest), I feel an empowered question mark. "I AM, what are we doing today?" I feel more like a ninja warrior on horseback than a middle-aged suburban woman on a laptop.

In Jeremiah 12, God tells the prophet (and servant), after he has been complaining to God about how everything is playing out, "If racing against mere men makes you tired, how will you race against horses? If you stumble and fall on open ground, what will you do in the thickets near the Jordan?" (Jeremiah 12:5 NLT). Because my "amazing" name *is* Jeremiah, I feel privileged to say to you what God is saying essentially to Jeremiah: "Get ready to run with horses." Let's run with horses, friends!

Alchemist

Alchemy is older than chemistry. In its original Greek form, alchemy literally means "to turn lead into gold."[7] Its more current definition (sadly often with a malicious connotation) is to turn the ordinary into something extraordinary. Doesn't the positive so sound like our God? In *The Alchemist* by Pablo Coelho, we find the young Andalusian shepherd Santiago, who, after having a dream while sleeping in an abandoned church, goes on a quest for his treasure (and purpose). He travels the world searching for wisdom among both good and bad people. Eventually he ends up right back where he started, with a fresh and spiritually full perspective, understanding that the treasure is within his heart. Along the journey, the alchemist in the story, someone who transforms things for the better, guides Santiago into wisdom. The alchemist says, "To realize one's destiny is a person's only obligation."[8]

In the prologue of the book, the author tells the story of Narcissus, the mythic tale of a man so mesmerized by his image in a lake that he fails to live his life and drowns. When the alchemist asks the lake about the image-obsessed man, the lake replies, "I weep for Narcissus, but I never noticed he was beautiful. I weep because, each time he knelt beside my banks, I could see, in the depths of his eyes, my own beauty reflected."[9]

Both tall tales are striking pictures of our path of life and how they might play out. We know there is a plan—a plan that we are a part of, to prosper us and not to harm us (Jeremiah 29:11). We are made in His image, a reflection of the glory of God (Ephesians 4:24). Are we like Santiago, willing to take a journey that will lead to the heart of the matter, our hearts? Or are we like Narcissus, obsessed with our image, unwilling to "go there," acting like all is well, never living out our stories and what God designed and reflected in us all along? St. Irenaeus reminds us that the "glory of God is human beings who are fully alive."

The ultimate alchemist is God, who is more than able to take something ordinary and turn it into something extraordinary (Ephesians 3:20)! Through sanctification and the renewing of your mind (Romans 12:2), He transforms you into the purpose-filled creation of His original design—the you that you always were from origin! Rescued! For your destiny!

Be Alert

"Objects in mirror are closer than they appear." When we see this phrase on most modern cars' side mirrors, we rarely consider it. Because the mirrors are slightly convex, they give us an increased range of vision. In fact, defensive driving instructors suggest the safest way to operate your moving vehicle is to glance at all three mirrors, rearview included, every five seconds. This is the sure way to avoid accidents as you drive to your destination. Apparently, not only is our short-term memory really short, but outside situations and conditions can change quickly too. Isn't that much like life?

As we have journeyed together and met some of the precious souls at The Lamb Center, I hope you have taken time to assess some of the things you see in your side mirrors of life—societal and cultural influences, family patterns, and even church choices and influences ("destiny derailers" in Figure #4). I hope you have examined the things in your rearview mirror—the left-behind parts of you that need rescuing. And I hope you are also keeping your eyes on the road ahead as you deal with conflict resolution in relationships, addictions, and the mess of cover-up.

"Kyrie Eleison!" This is not easy, but it's well worth it. The benefit of feeling wretched, miserable, poor, blind, and naked (Revelation 3:17) is that you can ask Jesus, as He counsels, to give you healing salve for your eyes to help you see (Revelation 3:18). He gives clarity to see, not just your neediness of Him and your truest reality, but also His exquisite and perfect help for you to be all He created you to be.

> "God opposes the proud but shows favor to the humble." (1 Peter 5:5)

As we continue to strip away image and go into the heart of the matter, we can better imagine and answer God's questions of "Where are you?" and "Where are you going?"

Joy to the World

To end where we began, I must talk about Joy. Yes, my joyful spirit. *And* also the human Joy, my daughter—the impetus to my entry into The Lamb Center. In her senior year of high school, amid such hardship and heart struggle, my progeny wrote a thirty-page senior thesis. In this age when public schools can run amuck with every gamut of every philosophy, her Christian high school did it right. They required her to prove what she believed, to defend her essentials of faith. Then she had to pick a complicated topic from our complicated society and defend her position (sound judgment). Then, she had to talk about her calling, or *vocare*. She had to write about what God might be speaking into her heart regarding her destiny. Oh, that I would have had a smidge of this assignment long, long ago!

My then quiet, studious daughter, crippled with fear and anxiety, worked on this endlessly. She was driven, wrestling with God for answers. She defended her thesis before the principal and administrators of the high school. There were fifteen finalists because there were so many excellent theses (such hope to our future generations, my friends). These students had to attend a debate moderated by the headmaster, who would judge the finalists and announce the winner at graduation. My daughter almost did not go to that final debate, figuring the image-laden folks at her school who won everything would win this highest award too. I insisted she go and be the real her. All of Joy with all of God, even in her struggle.

Graduation day, during a deluge of rain, we met at a local church to ceremoniously launch these seniors into the "real world." Family members and friends gathered. Awards were given — so many — to athletes, musicians, and scholars, to high-scorers and scholarship recipients.

Smiling at the hard work and dedication I knew Joy had endured, I beamed and clapped as she joined the fifteen finalists asked to stand and be recognized for their exemplary theses. Surely another would win, but then . . . "And the winner of the C.S. Lewis Award is . . . Joy Jeremiah!" An eternal spring of tears burst forth from me and a whole row of proud family members. Go, Joy, go!

Go, *you,* go! *Do* your destiny. In the midst of hardship and difficulty. Be the full you God designed. The reflection twinkling in His eye as the great I AM imagines you. Be all He needs you to be, and do all He needs you to do in this world that is in such desperate need of help, light, and truth. *Go* and be amazing you, with your amazing God!

Imagine!

Questions to Ponder:

1. For what do you say, "Lord, have mercy!"?
2. Have you experienced or do you experience the hamster wheel, or "meh," of life? Explain.
3. If you work with a charity, explain some of the things you have done to contribute.
4. Describe people you have seen finding their "groove."
5. Wrap your mind around Psalm 139. Read it together. What is most outstanding to you?
6. What do you think about the Parable of the Talents? Give real life examples.
7. What kinds of image have you noticed and/or stripped since beginning this book?
8. How have you more clearly heard the voice of God as you walk on your path of life?
9. Discuss the destiny derailers. What are you noticing? What about the side mirrors?
10. Let's have it! What is *amazing* about you?!
11. What is going on in your life that looks less than "destiny" material?
12. What is something in your past you need to explore as you move forward in your life?
13. Where do you get a glimpse of your destiny in the body of Christ?
14. What is God telling you about you—your life, your calling, your destiny?
15. How do your calling, your talents, and your gifts align with the world's deep hunger?
16. What steps will you take to become all of you, seeking and knowing all of God?

Let I AM IN to the heart of the matter.
Strip IMAGE. IMAGINE your destiny with God!

Acknowledgments

*T*hank you to the friends and leadership at The Lamb Center for sharing your stories in authenticity. By being real amid difficulty, your transformed hearts helped me see my broken self as beautiful. Your stories of redemption and restoration invited me into real life and real service. The welcoming spirit at The Lamb Center allowed me to volunteer in capacities of importance, which empowered me. I am ever grateful. The Holy Spirit shines brightly in that sacred place. Jesus' hands and feet are at work in that mighty place of God.

I am grateful to my sweet friends who were faithful during this process:

Judy, listening editor and friend, you were there from the beginning of the discovery of my story.

Joy, encourager, editor, friend, and teacher, our weekly times of dinner and friendship carried me through this lonely season. No wonder my mother adored you!

Thank you to all the friends and family who prayed for this book from its infancy, especially Brother Lawrence, who told me he prayed even more for this book than his own sermons. God bless you.

Rescued for Destiny – Joel 2 Army friends, you prayed and encouraged when no one else was near. Sherry and the whole group, you are valiant prayer warriors. I am indebted to your faithfulness.

Karen, there is no other woman more selfless and God-fearing than you. I am honored to call you sister and privileged to call you friend. Your contributions to the content were invaluable. Additionally, your countless hours of prayer, encouragement, editing, and pushing pressed *Imagine* to the finish line. You will have heavy crowns in heaven for your work to get me to my destiny. You are a true pioneer.

Douglas, cousin extraordinaire, artist and encourager, thank you for sharing your skills and caring for my heart.

Karla, your passion for justice put my feet on firm ground. Thank you for sharing your skills and your heart for others.

Doris, Brittany, and Gina, thank you for your eagle eye in editing and your encouragement.

Family. I know this wasn't easy. I love you. Thank you, Jamie. You gave me time, space, love, and dinners to get this done well. Your vulnerability to grow and expose our story to help others is brave and honorable. Your loyalty is steadying.

Dylan, precious son, thank you for your words of encouragement, especially at the very beginning when I thought this wouldn't be. You said, "Aren't you excited to be an author?" I had no idea I even had a book in me. You saw me at the end of the journey when it was just beginning. You dream big and encourage others to do the same. Mom B's countenance of encouragement lives on in your eyes.

Joy, your fearless push toward wellness in the face of discouragement and obstacles is an inspiration. You have no idea the places your courage brought me. I will ever thank you, the Joy in my life. You pursue God despite His occasional silence. You inspire me with your passionate belief when prayers are years in the answering. Your faithfulness will change the world. It has certainly changed mine.

God, thank You for speaking *Imagine* into my heart, and telling me to write. I loved co-creating with You! True Author and Finisher of my faith, thank You. You are trustworthy and true. There is none other worthy of more adoration than You. Lord, *You* are my great reward.

Appendix

Salvation Prayer:

> Lord Jesus, I need You. Thank You for dying on the cross for my sins. I open the door of my life and receive You as my Savior and Lord. Thank You for forgiving my sins and giving me eternal life. Take control of the throne of my life. Make me the kind of person You want me to be. Amen.[1]

Be sure to *tell* someone you prayed this prayer (Romans 10:9).

Prayer of Corporate Confession:

> Most holy and merciful Father, we acknowledge and confess before you our sinful nature, our shortcomings, and offenses. You alone know how often we have sinned in wandering from your way, in wasting your gifts, and in forgetting your love. Have mercy upon us, O Lord, who are ashamed and sorry for all that displeases you. Teach us to hate our errors, cleanse us from our secret faults, and forgive our sins for the sake of Jesus Christ, your own dear Son. Speak afresh to us the gospel of your grace, and remind us that if we confess our sins, you are faithful and just to forgive our sins and cleanse

us from all unrighteousness. In your Son is our salvation, in your promises our hope. Take us for your children and give us the spirit of your Son, and in the end receive us into your glory, through Jesus Christ our only Savior. Amen.[2]

Notes

Note from the Author:
1. *J2A Boot Camp: Christian Culture, God's Rest, and Active Participation.* By Sherry Colley and Karen Duckett. Culpeper, VA: April 2016.

Chapter One:
1. Ibid.

Chapter Two:
1. Leonard Mlodinow. "Henri Tajfel, "Experiments in Intergroup Discrimination," Scientific American, 1970." In *Subliminal: How Your Unconscious Mind Rules Your Behavior*. New York: Vintage Books, 2013.

Chapter Three:
1. Stormie Omartian. *The Power of a Praying Wife*. Eugene, OR: Harvest House Publishers, 2017.
2. Dan B. Allender, and Tremper Longman. *The Cry of the Soul: How Our Emotions Reveal Our Deepest Questions about God*. Colorado Springs, CO: NavPress, 2015.
3. Ibid.

Chapter Five:
1. Beth Moore. *Living beyond Yourself: Exploring the Fruit of the Spirit*. Nashville, TN: LifeWay Press, 2004.

Chapter Six:
1. National Coalition for the Homeless. "Mental Illness and Homelessness." News release, July 2009. http://www. nationalhomeless.org/factsheets/Mental_Illness.html.

2. Dan B. Allender. *To Be Told: Know Your Story, Shape Your Life*. Colorado Springs, CO: Waterbrook Press, 2005.
3. John Friel, and Linda Friel. *An Adult Child's Guide to What's Normal*. Deerfield Beach, FL: Health Communications, Inc., 2010.
4. Karen Duckett. *"Rescued for Destiny Basics,"* 2013.
5. Louis Cozolino. "The Neuroscience of Human Relationships." *The Neuropsychotherapist*. January 17, 2013. Accessed October 24, 2017. http://www.neuropsychotherapist.com/review-the-neuroscience-of-human-relationships/.
6. Harvard Review Psychiatry. *The Body Keeps the Score*. 1994, 36.

Chapter Seven:
1. Emma Lazarus. *New Colossus,* 1883.
2. John Eldredge. *The Journey of Desire: Searching for the Life You've Always Dreamed of*. Nashville, TN: Nelson Books, an Imprint of Thomas Nelson, 2016.
3. Ibid.

Chapter Eight:
1. Seuss. *Oh, the Places You'll Go!* London: HarperCollins Children's Books, 2016.
2. Jan Karon. *At Home in Mitford*. New York, NY: G.P. Putnam's Sons, 2017.

Chapter Nine:
1. *Restoration of the Heart*. By Dan Allender and John Eldredge. Colorado Springs, CO: May 2016.

Chapter Ten:
1. "Judging." In *The Merriam-Webster Dictionary*. Springfield, MA: Merriam-Webster, Incorporated, 2016.
2. Paul Tripp. *New Morning Mercies: A Daily Gospel Devotional*. Wheaton, IL: Crossway, 2014.

Chapter Eleven:
1. Darryl McCollum. "In All Things Grace: A Layman's Take on Church Unity (Hardback)." *In All Things*

Grace. July 08, 2015. Accessed October 24, 2017. https://www.waterstones.com/book/in-all-things-grace/ darryl-mccollum/9781490883113.

2. Josh Packard and Ashleigh Hope. *Church Refugees: Sociologists Reveal Why People Are Done with the Church but Not Their Faith*. Loveland, CO: Group, 2015.
3. Ibid.
4. James Emery White. *The Rise of the Nones: Understanding and Reaching the Religiously Unaffiliated*. Grand Rapids, MI: Baker Books, 2014.
5. Nicky Gumbel. "About." Got Questions - Try Alpha. Accessed October 24, 2017. https://alphausa.org/about.
6. Lonnie Lane. "Messianic Vision." "Church" Isn't in the New Testament" - Sid Roth's Messianic Vision. Accessed October 24, 2017. http://srmv.convio.net/site/News2?abbr=art_&id=8657.
7. Ibid.
8. Rick Joyner. *Visions of the Harvest*. Fort Mill, SC: MorningStar Publications, 2008.

Chapter Twelve:
1. Howard Macy. *Rhythms of the Inner Life*. Newberg, OR: Red Nose Fun Publishing, LLC, 2012.
2. John Eldredge and Brent Curtis. *The Sacred Romance*. Nashville, TN: Thomas Nelson, Inc., 1997.
3. Frederick Buechner. *Wishful Thinking: A Seeker's ABC*. London: Mowbray, 1994, 95.
4. Ibid.
5. David G. Benner. *Desiring God's Will: Aligning Our Hearts with the Heart of God*. Downers Grove, IL: IVP Books, 2015.
6. Ibid.
7. Paulo Coelho. *The Alchemist: 25th Anniversary Edition*. New York, NY: HarperCollins Publishers, 2014.
8. Ibid.
9. Ibid.

Appendix

1. Bill Bright. "Knowing God Personally." Cru.org. 2015. Accessed October 24, 2017. https://www.cru.org/how-to-know-god/would-you-like-to-know-god-personally.html.
2. Robert Norris. "Fourth Presbyterian Church." Fourth Presbyterian Church. Accessed October 24, 2017. http://4th-pres.org/.

About the Author

*D*eeAnn Jeremiah is an author, speaker, and teacher whose enthusiasm for following God and fulfilling her destiny inspires others to do the same.

As an entrepreneur and business woman, she founded Washington DC-area-based Classic Concierge in 1989. Based on servant leadership principles, it is now a thriving customer service and event company. Her communication style and warmth make her an effective leader and teacher, inspiring others to serve and live well. Her experience following God spans nearly thirty years as discussion and music leader, facilitator and teacher of various Bible studies. Most recently, DeeAnn's passion for teaching groups about abundant living emerged from her love for the poor and poor in spirit while teaching weekly Bible Study at The Lamb Center, a homeless day shelter, where she currently serves on the Board. She is a member of the Capital Speakers Club, a group of empowered women sharing life and wisdom through the art of public speaking.

DeeAnn's thirst for adventure and exercise in the great outdoors fills her with excitement and delight. Because nature *is* God's original Bible, she can barely stand to be inside, but if she must, it is to invite others into conversations and connection, through counseling and prayer. Other loves include nature photography, singing, piano, and gardening (especially for the dirt, birds, and butterflies). Her biggest reward is spending quality time with friends and family.

DeeAnn is *most* passionate about the life change possible by becoming all of the real you and knowing all of the real God—the full measure of JOY!

If you would like to know more about
The Lamb Center or
make a contribution,
please visit their website at
www.thelambcenter.org.

More at
www.DeeAnnPlusGod.com

CPSIA information can be obtained
at www.ICGtesting.com
Printed in the USA
BVHW03s2026220218
508882BV00001B/1/P